Country Gi

Modern

11 Modern-Traditional Quilts from the Junction

By Jo Kramer
and Kelli Hanken

Country Girl Modern

11 Modern-Traditional Quilts from the Junction

By Jo Kramer and Kelli Hanken

Editor: Jenifer Dick
Designer: Sarah Meiers
Photography: Aaron T. Leimkuehler
Illustration: Logan Wright
Technical Editor: Beth Burke
Photo Editor: Jo Ann Groves

Published by:
Kansas City Star Books
1729 Grand Blvd.
Kansas City, Missouri, USA 64108

First edition, first printing
ISBN: 978-1-61169-153-5

Kansas City Star Quilts moves quickly to publicize corrections to our books. You can find corrections at www.KansasCityStarQuilts.com, then click on "Corrections."

Library of Congress Control Number: 2014958252

Printed in the United States of America by Walsworth Publishing Co., Marceline, MO

To order copies, call StarInfo at (816) 234-4473.

KANSAS CITY STAR QUILTS
Continuing the Tradition
KansasCityStarQuilts.com

My Stars
a new tradition
MyStarsBlog.com

Contents

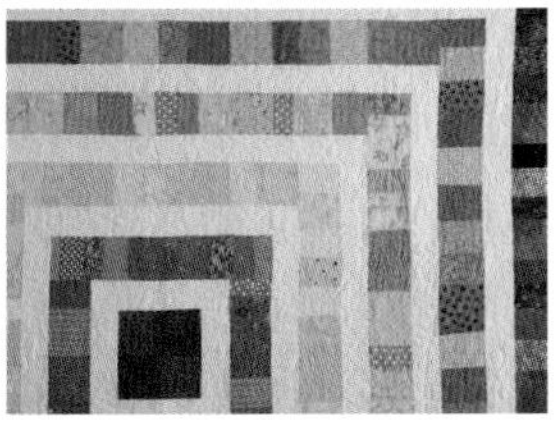
Rainbow Connection 10

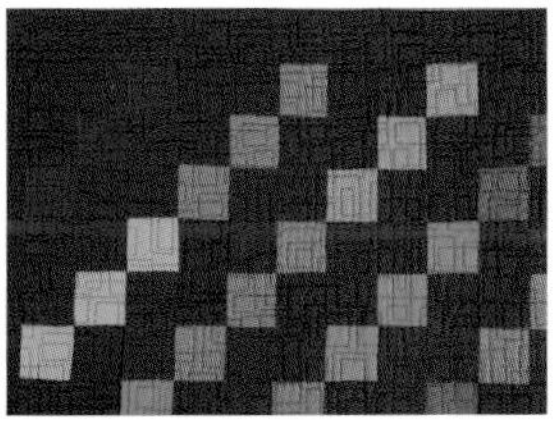
Almost Amish 18

Connect Four 26

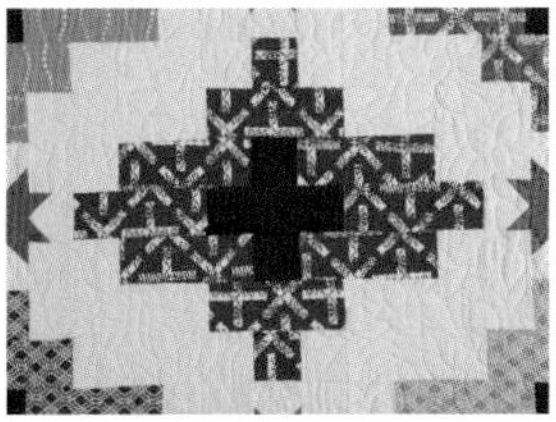
May Flowers 34

Bohemian Rhapsody 46

Modern Day Patriot 52

Puddle Duck 64

Modalicious 74

Pilot Knob 84

School Bus 92

Thanks to YOU! 102

Dedication

This book, our first published book, is for the generations of quilters in our family. We are so thankful that their labors of love have evolved into an enriching and entertaining hobby for both of us. From the quilt made from a blanket factory's silk binding scraps, to the quilt made with 30s prints and bubblegum pink solids, to the calico appliqué farm scene quilts — made by generations past — we treasure them all.

We think especially of Evalonne Johnson, our mother and grandmother, who we lost too soon. She was a whiz with fabric and could truly make wonderful things out of simple scraps. She was especially talented with a seam ripper as she ripped out many mistakes of those she taught to sew.

We also think of our Aunt Agnes, who at 96 years old continues to sew quilts and donates them through Lutheran World Relief. Many, many people around the world have been blessed with quilts that her hands have touched.

We are very blessed to be following in some mighty big shoes.

Acknowledgments

Our journey to publishing this book began back in 2010 when we submitted a quilt pattern idea to Moda Bake Shop. It was on a whim and we never imagined we'd have a project selected for publication but we did. We were so happy.

That started our wonderful relationship with the folks at Moda Fabrics. They have been helpful every step of the way throughout our journey sharing their fabric, contacts and encouragement.

Much of the fabric you see throughout this book is courtesy of Moda. From Lissa to the people in the sample room managing our requests, we thank you.

We have other fabric companies to thank as well: Free Spirit supplied the fabric for Bohemian Rhapsody and Andover for May Flowers. Your fabrics made our quilts sing and we thank you for that.

We would also like to thank Kayla, our daughter and sister. It was Kayla who gave us the push to submit our proposal to Kansas City Star Quilts. Without her encouragement, we don't think we would have been brave enough to try writing a book. Kayla was also the person who encouraged us to start a blog. For some reason she thought it would be a good fit for us, and it truly is.

Our blog readers also deserve a big thanks. After about our 15th pattern with Moda Bake Shop, a reader left a comment that said, "OK — it is time for you girls to write a book." That comment planted the seed.

Thanks to our many day-to-day readers — without you we would be just a voice in the wind. We cannot believe how many friends we have made through the blog and what a blessing those friends are. A special thanks goes to Michelle over at Michelle's Romantic Tangle, www.mychellem.blogspot.com. You've been there for us at all times of the night and day offering advice and encouragement plus putting up with our drama. It is great that we can be us with you. We cannot wait to meet you in person one day.

We thank Ila too. You've adopted us in a way that no one else could. We look forward to your emails and the boxes that the FedEx man delivers. We only wish we could do something in return for all the wonderful gifts you have sent our way.

Thanks to Doug Weaver at Kansas City Star Books for giving these two Iowa gals a chance. Thanks also to the cast and crew at Kansas City Star for bringing our vision of the book to life. You are great to work with Jenifer Dick, Sarah Meiers, Aaron Leimkuehler, Logan Wright, Beth Burke and Jo Ann Groves. We hope this is the beginning of a long-lasting relationship.

From Jo

Acknowledgments are always so hard for me to write. Where does a person start? Do I thank my first grade teacher, Mrs. Westing, for giving me a "unsatisfactory" in the "using my time wisely" category, which encouraged me to open my eyes to be more efficient? I do thank her and the countless others who have touched me along the way. But I mostly want to thank my family. My kids are amazingly supportive and they learned that from their dad. He has a special talent in that he can keep me grounded yet give me wings to soar. What more does a girl need? Thanks, Honey!

From Kelli

I would like to thank my wonderful husband, Jason, for loving me in a house that isn't always perfectly tidy, eating the occasional frozen pizza suppers and putting up with my wonderful mood when stressed. Without your understanding, this publication would not be possible.

Thank you also to my wonderful dog, Puppycat. I know she cannot read or understand this, but having her to pet or snuggle really helps to clear my head, take a step back, and to try again.

To you all, we thank you.

Foreword

Sewing With Family

As a mother-daughter team we are always asked questions like: "How do you sew together?" We thought we would pass along what has worked for us.

From Kelli

1. If your mom offers to buy or gift you with something to help you sew, accept it. Even if it's not your favorite color or in the best shape, chances are it will work until you know what you want to buy for yourself.
2. Shop your mom's fabric and notions first.
3. Precuts are a great option when you do not have a stash of fabric.
4. Try Mom's way, and if that does not work, try your own.
5. Remember that you are not just building a quilt. You are building memories.

Jo (left) and Kelli with their beagles, Gracie and Puppycat.

From Jo

1. Provide a working machine and the right equipment. It doesn't need to be fancy.
2. Let them sew — you do the ripping.
3. Pick projects for success. Rainbow Connection (page 10) is a good option.
4. If you aren't patient enough to teach your children, send them to "Aunt Judy" (I did) or to the local quilt shop for lessons.
5. If your daughter makes you something that is hideous — like a table runner in colors that are not your favorite, with a variety of thread colors and binding that is turned over so poorly that batting is sticking out and the raw edges show — tell her you love it. Tell her you cannot believe how hard she worked to make something so very special. Show her how beautifully (one of) the corners fit together. Tell her you didn't even know she could machine quilt.

When your friends come to visit, show them the amazing and wonderful table runner that your daughter made just for you. Tell them the table runner is so special that you do not keep it in the kitchen where it can get ruined. Tell them you keep it on the dresser in your bedroom so nothing will get spilled on it. Tell them you keep it there so that every night before you go to bed, you can remember how blessed you are to have a daughter who would work so hard to make such an incredible gift.

My daughter Kalissa surprised me with this creation when she was 10. I still treasure it.

"The" table runner!

Rainbow Connection

Finished Size: 70 ½" × 70 ½"

Whenever I see rainbows I think of Kermit the Frog singing "The Rainbow Connection" from "The Muppet Movie." That is the premise of this quilt — just connect the rainbows of fabric scraps!

When Kelli was growing up, she loved to play in the scrap bin. Not much has changed. We start quilts by making a mess of our scrap bin. Rainbow Connection is a great quilt for "fabric petters" like us. We started out by sorting out piles of red, orange, yellow, blue, green and purple scraps. Of course conversations started: "Oh this scrap was from this project and this scrap was from that project..."

This beginner-friendly quilt can be completed with no seams to match. It is great practice for cutting even strips and sewing straight seams. Just dig out your scrap bin (or dive into your mom's) and start cutting 3 ½" wide strips. You can do it!

Fabric Requirements

2¼ yards Neutral background

1 yard total assorted Red prints

½ yard total assorted Orange prints

½ yard total assorted Yellow prints

½ yard total assorted Green prints

¾ yard total assorted Turquoise prints

¾ yard total assorted Purple prints

¾ yard total Turquoise scraps for binding

4 yards backing

Cutting Instructions

From Neutral fabric:
Cut 27 — 2½″ × width-of-fabric strips

From Red fabric:
Cut 4 — 3½″ squares

From EACH colored fabric:
Cut 3½″ strips of varying lengths ranging from 2½″ to 6½″

You will need enough to make the following lengths of each color:

Orange: 54″
Yellow: 94″
Green: 134″
Turquoise: 174″
Purple: 214″
Red: 268″

From Turquoise fabric:
Cut scraps into 2½″ × various length strips.

Sewing Instructions

Background Strips
With right sides together, sew all of the neutral background fabric strips together.

Center Four-Patch
With right sides together, sew 2 sets of 2 red 3½" squares. Press. Sew the 2 sets of squares together to make a 4-patch unit.

[Make 1 — 6½" unfinished red four-patch unit]

Pieced Strips
For each color, join all of the cut pieces of various lengths together on the 3½" side and press in one direction, making sure that you have at least 54" of orange, 94" of yellow, 134" of green, 174" of blue, 214" of purple and 268" of red.

NOTE: When joining the 3½" segments, it is extremely important to sew with an accurate ¼" seam allowance. This will ensure that your strips are free of puckers and waves that may occur with an inaccurate seam allowance.

Top Assembly

From the 2½" neutral background strip, cut 2 pieces that are 6½" long and 2 pieces that are 10½" long. With right sides together, sew the 6½" rectangles to opposite sides of the red four-patch square. Press to the neutral. Repeat using the 10½" rectangles, sewing them to the opposite sides of the square. Again, press to the neutral.

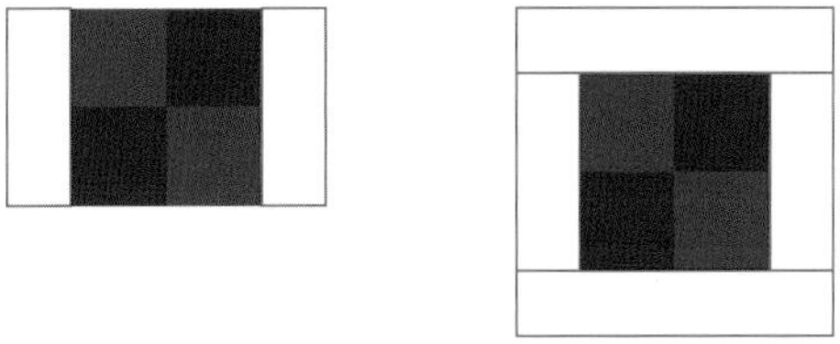

[10½" unfinished center unit]

Measure your neutral-framed red four-patch through the middle. Cut 2 pieces of the measured length from the orange 3½" strip. Sew to opposite sides of the framed red four-patch and press to the orange. Measure your resulting rectangle horizontally through the middle. Cut 2 pieces of the measured length from the orange 3½" strip. Sew these pieces, right sides together, to the opposite long sides of your rectangle and press to the orange.

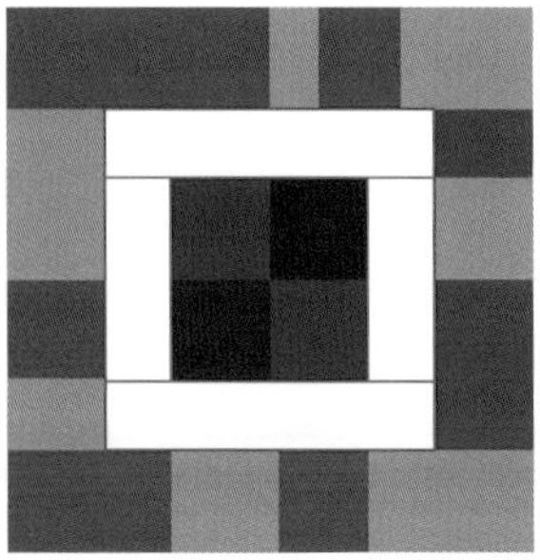

Measure your orange-framed square through the middle. Cut 2 pieces of the measured length from the neutral background fabric strip. Sew to opposite sides of the square and press to the neutral. Measure your rectangle horizontally through the middle. Cut 2 pieces of the measured length from the neutral background. Sew these pieces, right sides together, to the opposite long sides of your rectangle and press to the neutral.

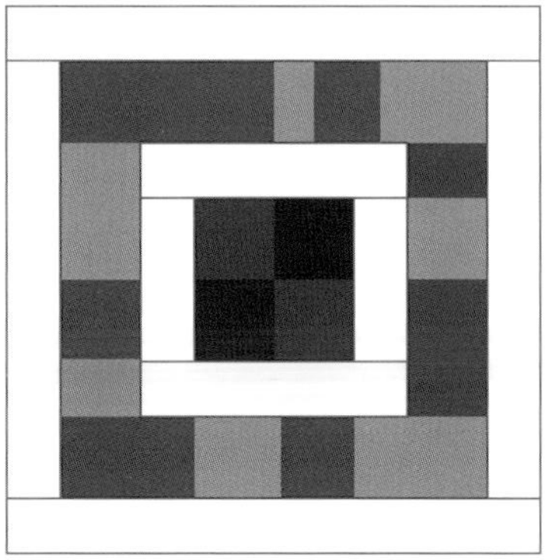

Continue adding colors in this manner until you have added 6 colors, each with a frame of neutral strips.

[Quilt Assembly Diagram]

Finishing

Quilting

Layer the backing, batting and top. Quilt as desired. We used a white thread and an edge-to-edge design from The Pajama Quilter. (See resources page 112.)

Binding

Join the scrappy binding strips on the diagonal creating 300″ of binding. Bind the quilt.

Almost Amish

Finished Block Size: 6"
Finished Quilt Size: 64½" × 76½"

We were inspired to make a quilt with solid colors after a recent trip to an Amish community near our home. A family had a clothesline pulley strung between their back door and the top of a silo. The simple beauty of a family's clothes, all in beautiful jewel tones, impressed us. Typically Amish quilts feature black backgrounds with jewel-toned solids. We made our quilt a bit different by changing the black background to brown.

We found a beautiful print for our backing fabric that inspired our color selection for the quilt top. This strip-pieced quilt couldn't be any simpler!

Fabric Requirements

4 yards Brown solid background

½ yard Yellow solid

½ yard Coral solid

½ yard Orange solid

½ yard Light Brown solid

½ yard Pink solid

½ yard Green solid

½ yard Turquoise solid

¾ yard Turquoise binding

5½ yards backing

Cutting Instructions

From Brown background:

Cut 25 — 2½" × width-of-fabric strips

- Subcut 3 strips into 14 — 2½" × 6" rectangles
- Of the remaining strips, 14 will be used in block construction and 8 will be used in the border

Cut 17 — 4½" × width-of-fabric strips

- Subcut 3 strips into 7 — 4½" × 11" segments

From EACH solid color:

Cut a total of 4 — 2½" × width-of-fabric strips

- Subcut one strip into 1 — 2½" × 6" segment and 1 — 2½" × 11" segment
- The remaining 3 strips of each color will be used in block construction

From Turquoise:

Cut 8 — 2½" × width-of-fabric strips for binding

[Quick Reference Chart]

1

Segment A
1 per block

2

Segment B
2 per block

3

6½" × 6½" unfinished
120 total units

Sewing Instructions

BLOCKS

Segment A

With right sides together, sew one of each of the colored 2½" × width-of-fabric strips to a brown 2½" × width-of-fabric strip along their lengths. Also join each of the colored 2½" × 6" rectangles to a brown 2½" × 6" rectangle along their long sides. Press to the brown. Sew a second brown strip to the opposite side of each of the colored strips on both the width-of-fabric unit and the 6" unit. Press to the brown. Cut each long strip set into 16 — 2½" segments and each short segment into 2 — 2½" segments for a total of 18 segments.

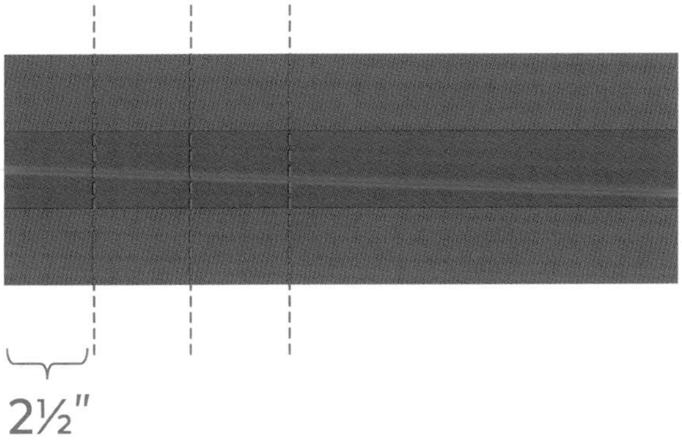

[Segment A — Make 1 segment per block]

Segment B

Sew a colored 2½" × width-of-fabric strip to a brown 4½" × width-of-fabric strip. Make 2 of each color. Also sew each colored 2½" × 11" strip to a brown 4½" × 11" strip. Press to the brown. Cut each long strip set into 16 — 2½" segments. Cut each short strip set into 4 — 2½" segments for a total of 36 — 2½" segments of each color.

[Segment B — Make 2 segments per block]

Block

Sew a Segment B to each side of a Segment A, ensuring that a diagonal pattern is formed with squares of the same color through each block. Make 18 blocks of each color. You need 120 blocks total for the quilt.

[Make 18 — 6½" unfinished blocks in each of the 7 colors]

NOTE: You will make 126 total blocks, but only 120 are needed for the quilt.

Top Assembly

Assemble the quilt top in a 10 × 12, barn-raising layout as shown with colors evenly distributed throughout the quilt.

Borders

Join the 8 — 2½" × width-of-fabric strips on the diagonal with right sides together. Measure your quilt vertically through the middle. Cut 2 brown border pieces to this measurement. Attach to sides of the quilt. Press to the brown border. Measure your quilt horizontally through the middle. Cut 2 brown border pieces to this measurement. Attach to the top and bottom of the quilt and press to the brown border.

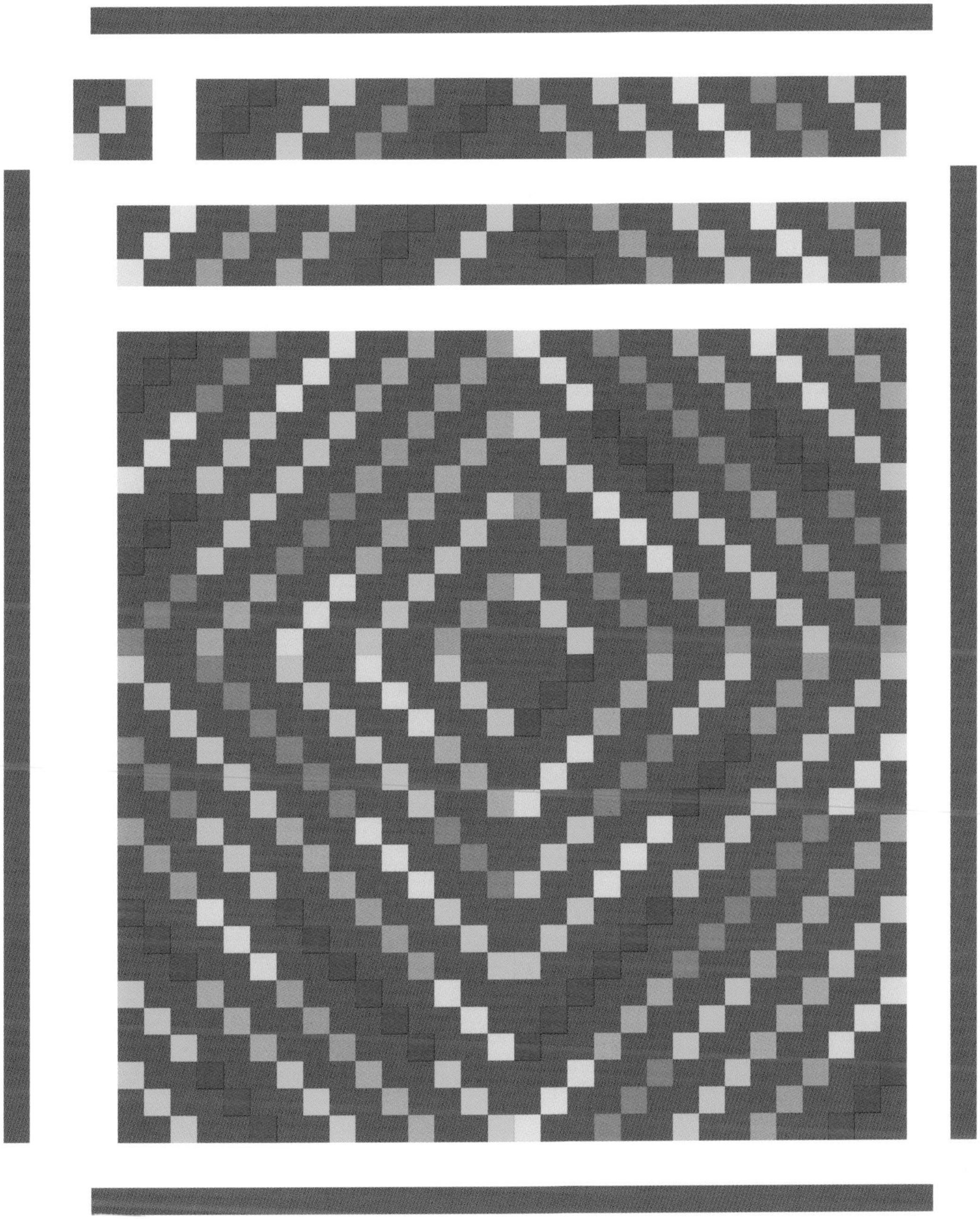

[Quilt Assembly Diagram]

Finishing

Quilting
Layer the backing, batting and top. Quilt as desired. We used a brown thread and a boxy overall edge-to-edge design.

Binding
Join the 8 turquoise binding strips on the diagonal and bind the quilt.

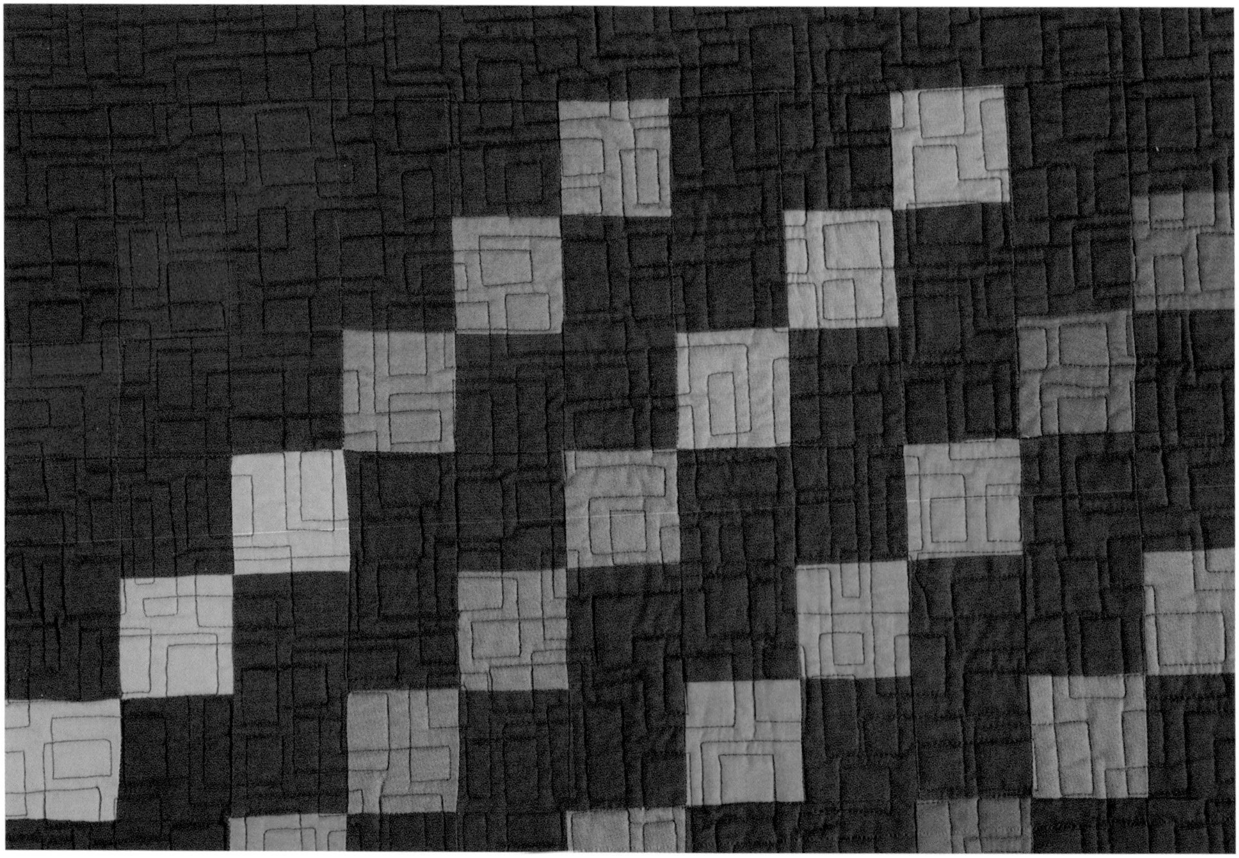

Almost Amish

Connect Four

Finished Block Size: 8″
Finished Quilt Size: 68½″ × 84½″

Connect Four was inspired by our love of pre-cuts. All too often, while visiting a quilt shop, we fall in love with a fabric line, but we don't have a project in mind so we just pick up two charm packs. Once home, we wonder what we're going to do with them. We designed this quilt knowing we aren't the only quilters with two matching charm packs waiting for inspiration.

Just like the classic children's game, winning is as simple as connecting four squares. The whole quilt is composed of only two blocks so it is quick to make. Choosing a dark blue as the background makes it a bit more masculine and therefore a great quilt for a boy. It is a favorite design of ours to donate to local benefits and charities, because the quilt comes together so quickly.

If you don't have charm packs, no worries. You can use up your 2½″ scraps on this project if you choose.

INTERNATIONAL HARVESTER

Fabric Requirements

2 charm packs
  OR a minimum of 80 — 5″ colored squares
  OR 320 — 2½″ squares

4½ yards Background fabric

¾ yard Red binding

4 yards backing

Cutting Instructions

From Background fabric:

Cut 15 — 8½″ × the width-of-fabric strips

- Subcut 7 strips into 40 — 6½″ × 8½″ rectangles
- Subcut 5 strips into 40 — 4½″ × 8½″ rectangles
- Subcut 3 strips into 40 — 2½″ × 8½″ rectangles

Cut 8 — 2½″ × width-of-fabric strips to be used for the border

From Red fabric:

Cut 8 — 2½″ × the width-of-fabric strips for binding

[Quick Reference Chart]

1	2	3
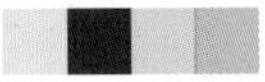		
80 total	Block A 8½″ × 8½″ unfinished 40 total	Block B 8½″ × 8½″ unfinished 40 total

Sewing Instructions

BLOCKS

TIP: When you begin making this quilt, it may be helpful to rearrange your charm packs a bit as they are often packaged with like colors close to each other. If you are using 2 charm packs of the same fabric line, you may want to throw them in a bowl to mix up the squares.

1 Select 2 – 5" charm squares. With right sides together, sew a ¼" seam on 2 of the opposite sides of the charm square set. Using a rotary cutter, cut vertically and horizontally through the middle of the charm square set.

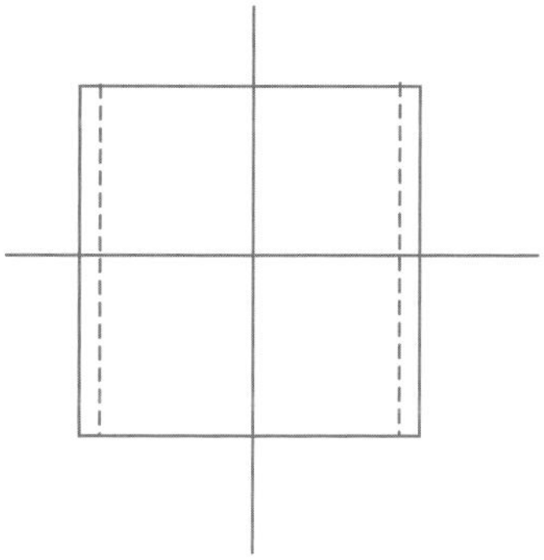

You will have 4 matching sets of 2 joined 2½" squares. Repeat with the remaining charm squares to make 160 pairs. Join 2 sets of pairs end to end to make 4 – 2½" squares in a row. Repeat to make 80 – 4-block rows.

NOTE: If you are using 2½" scraps, sew them into 80 sets of 4 squares in a row.

Block A

2 With right sides together, join 1 pieced row to a 6½" × 8½" background rectangle. Press to the background fabric. Repeat to make 40 blocks.

[Block A: Make 40 – 8½" unfinished]

Block B

3 Join 1 of the remaining 40 pieced rows to a 2½" × 8½" rectangle. Press to the background fabric. Join a 4½" × 8½" rectangle to the opposite side of the unit. Press to the background fabric.

[Block B: Make 40 – 8½" unfinished]

Top Assembly

4 Using 4 Block A and 4 Block B, create 10 horizontal rows as shown, rotating the blocks to create the pattern.

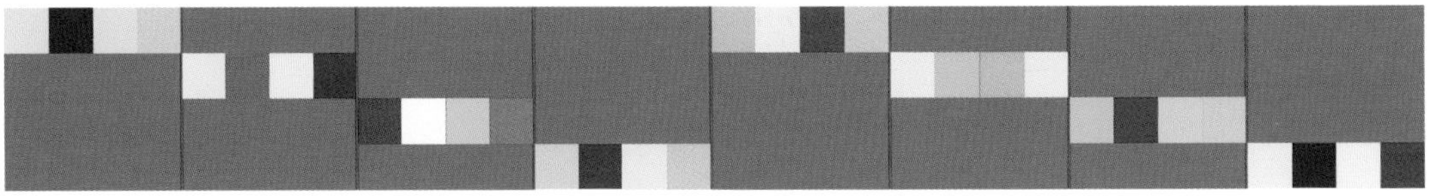

Borders

Measure your quilt vertically through the middle. Cut 2 border pieces to this measurement. Sew a border piece to both sides of the quilt. Press to the border. Measure your quilt horizontally through the middle. Cut 2 border pieces to this measurement. Sew a border piece to both the top and the bottom. Press to the border.

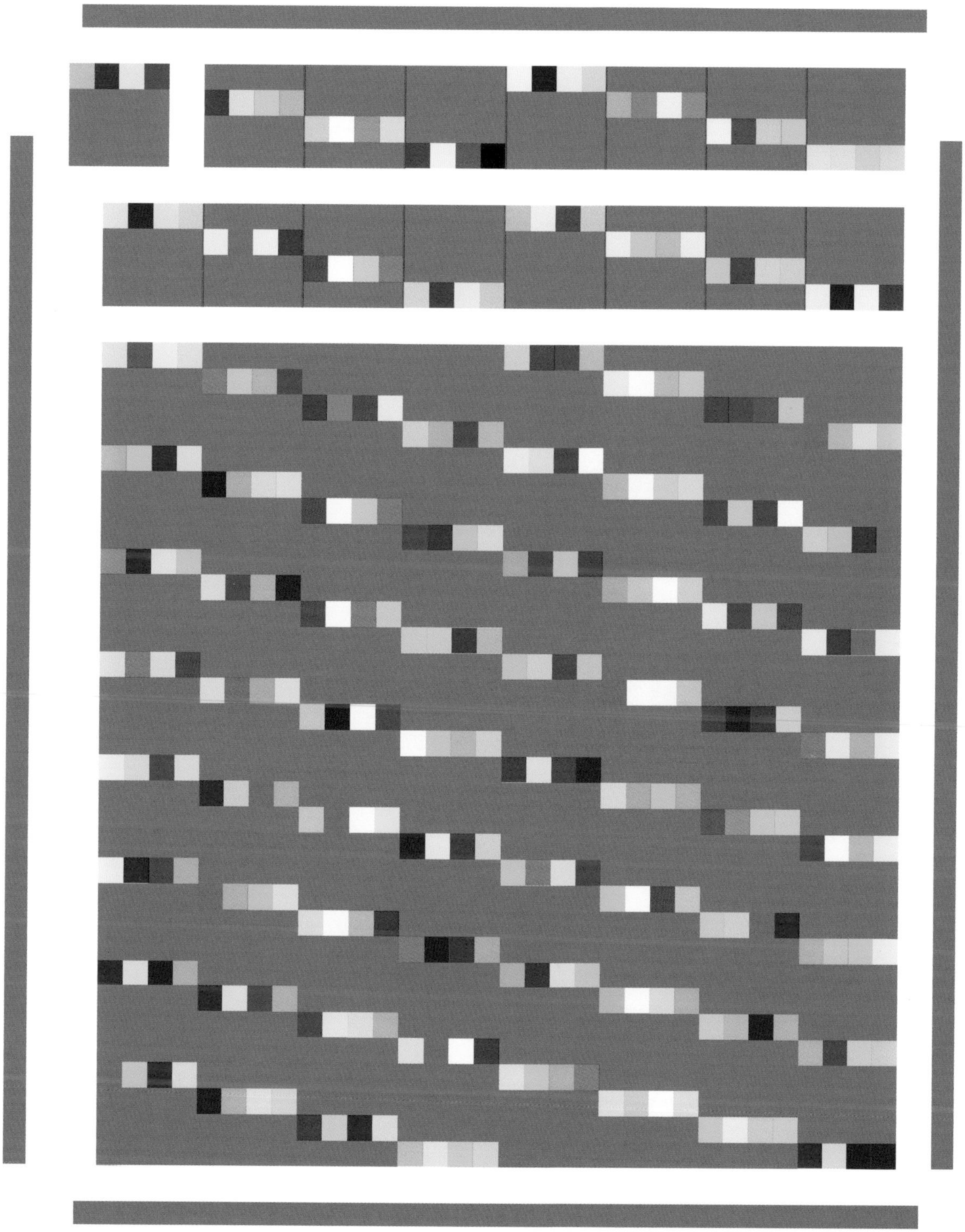

[Quilt Assembly Diagram]

Finishing

Quilting
Layer the backing, batting and top. Quilt as desired. We used a navy thread and a zigzag pattern from The Pajama Quilter (see resources page 112).

Binding
Join the 8 red binding strips on the diagonal and bind the quilt.

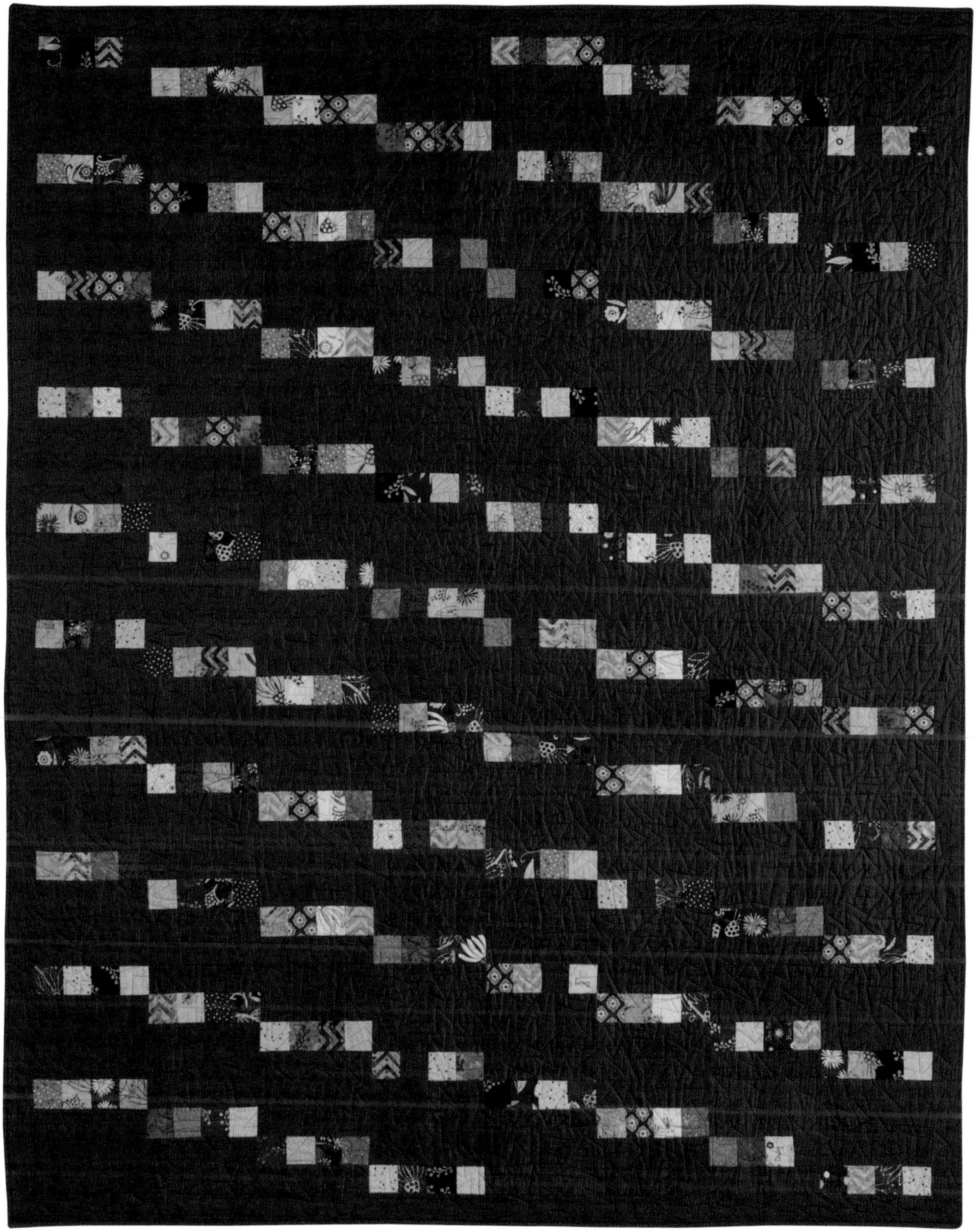

May Flowers

Finished Quilt Size:
98½" × 102½"

April has always been known to bring showers. While we worked on this quilt it rained and rained and rained, bringing more rain to our Midwest community than our farmer husbands needed. The forecast for days to come called for rain. Because the livelihood of a farming community greatly depends on the weather, the constant rain was frustrating the farmers and us.

We sewed through those dreary April days, waiting for the rain to stop and the promised May flowers to bloom. This design reminded us so much of flowers and brought us hope that the rains would soon end and that sunny days filled with May flowers were ahead.

Fabric Requirements

Approximately 7½ yards of up to 50 different colored prints — a minimum of 5" × width-of-fabric per color

¾ yard Blue print

2¼ yards Red solid

5½ yards White background

8 yards backing

Cutting Instructions

For EACH of the 32 colored middle blocks:

Cut 2 — 2½" × width-of-fabric strips

- Subcut 8 — 2½" × 6½" rectangles
- Subcut 2 — 2½" squares

For EACH of the 4 colored corner blocks:

Cut 1 — 2½" × width-of-fabric strip

- Subcut 2 — 2½" × 6½" rectangles
- Subcut 1 — 2½" × 4½" rectangle
- Subcut 1 — 2½" square

For EACH of the 6 colored top and bottom partial blocks:

Cut 1 — 2½" × width-of-fabric strip

- Subcut 5 — 2½" × 6½" rectangles
- Subcut 1 — 2½" square

For EACH of the 8 colored side partial blocks:

Cut 1 — 2½" × width-of-fabric strips

- Subcut 3 — 2½" × 6½" rectangles
- Subcut 2 — 2½" × 4½" rectangles
- Subcut 2 — 2½" squares

From Blue print:

Cut 2 — 2½" × width-of-fabric strips

- Subcut 31 — 2½" squares

Cut 10 — 1½" × width-of-fabric strips

- Subcut 248 — 1½" squares

From Red solid:

Cut 26 — 2½" × width-of-fabric strips

- Subcut 6 strips into 90 — 2½" squares
- Subcut 2 strips into 12 — 2½" × 4½" rectangles
- Subcut 7 strips into 38 — 2½" × 6½" rectangles
- The remaining 2½" strips will be used for binding

From White solid:

Cut 74 — 2½" × width-of-fabric strips

- Subcut 34 strips into 540 — 2½" squares
- Subcut 32 strips into 192 — 2½" × 6½" rectangles
- Subcut 8 strips into 60 — 2½" × 4½"rectangles

ORGANIZATIONAL NOTE: Keep each color separate and keep track of the full and partial blocks as you sew. It's easy to get the components mixed up. We suggest you refer to the assembly diagram and put the units on a design wall as you cut and sew them so you can easily see where each color goes.

Quick Reference Chart

1 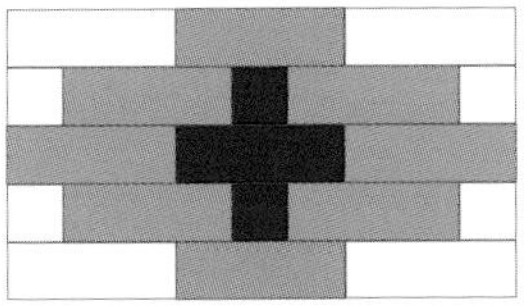 Middle Blocks 32 blocks	2  64 units 2 per middle block	3  Top and Bottom Partial Blocks 6 blocks
4 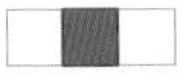 6 units 1 per top and bottom block	5 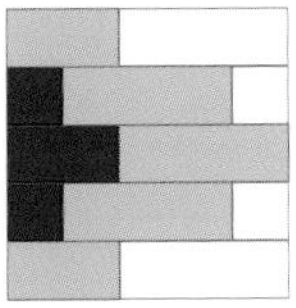 Side Partial Blocks 8 blocks	6  16 units 2 per partial block 4 units 1 per corner block
7 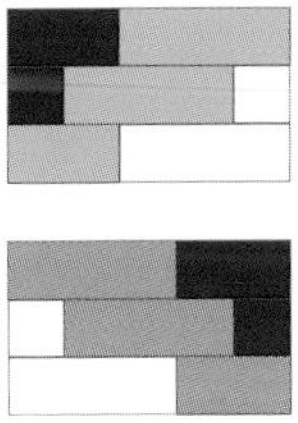 Corner Blocks 2 of each	8  124 units	9 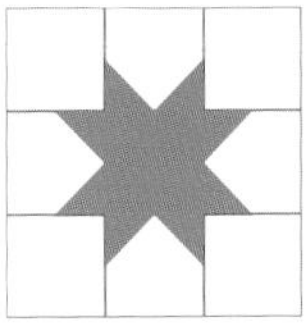 Star Block 31 blocks
10  Top and Bottom Connector Units 8 units	11  Side Connector Units 10 units	

Sewing Instructions

MAY FLOWERS BLOCKS

For each of the 32 colored middle blocks, you will need to create the following units:

Make 1 per block using:

2 — colored 2½" × 6½" rectangles
1 — red 2½" × 6½" rectangle

[Make 1 per block]

Make 2 per block using:

2 — white 2½" × 6½" rectangles
1 — colored 2½" × 6½" rectangle

[Make 2 per block]

Make 2 per block using:

2 — white 2½" squares
2 — colored 2½" × 6½" rectangles
1 — red 2½" square

[Make 2 per block]

1 Assemble each block as shown. Lay the units out and sew strips together to complete the block. Make 32 blocks.

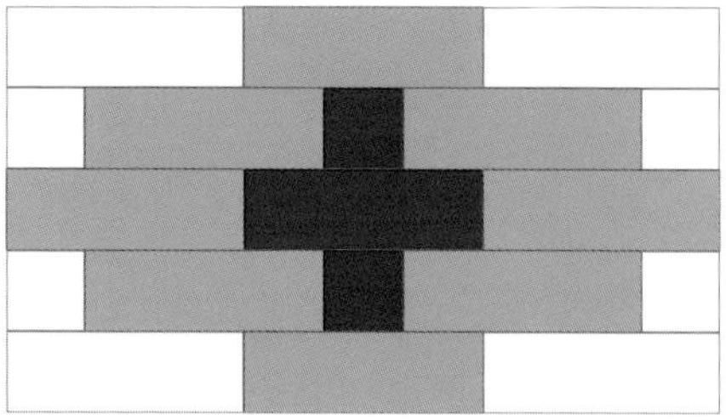

[Make 32 blocks]

STAR BLOCK TOP AND BOTTOM CONNECTORS

For each block, you will also need to make 2 Star Block Top and Bottom Connectors, which will be assembled later.

2 Attach 2 white 2½" squares to each side of 1 — 2½" colored square that you will be using for the 32 middle blocks. Make 2 per block. Set aside.

[Make 64 total — 2 per block]

TOP AND BOTTOM PARTIAL BLOCKS

To make the partial blocks for the top and bottom, you will need to create the following units for each of the 6 blocks:

- 2 colored 2½" × 6½" rectangles
- 1 red 2½" × 6½" rectangle

[Make 1 per block]

- 2 white 2½" squares
- 2 colored 2½" × 6½" rectangles
- 1 red 2½" square

[Make 1 per block]

- 2 white 2½" × 6½" rectangles
- 1 colored 2½" × 6½" rectangle

[Make 1 per block]

3 Lay the units out as pictured. Sew strips together to complete the block. Repeat to make 6 blocks.

[Make 6]

TOP AND BOTTOM CONNECTOR

For each top and bottom partial block, you will also need to make 1 Star Block Connector, which will be assembled later.

4 Attach a white 2½" square to each of the 2½" colored squares that you will be using for the 6 top and bottom blocks. Set aside.

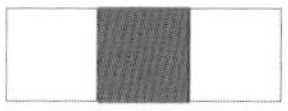

[Make 6 — 1 per block]

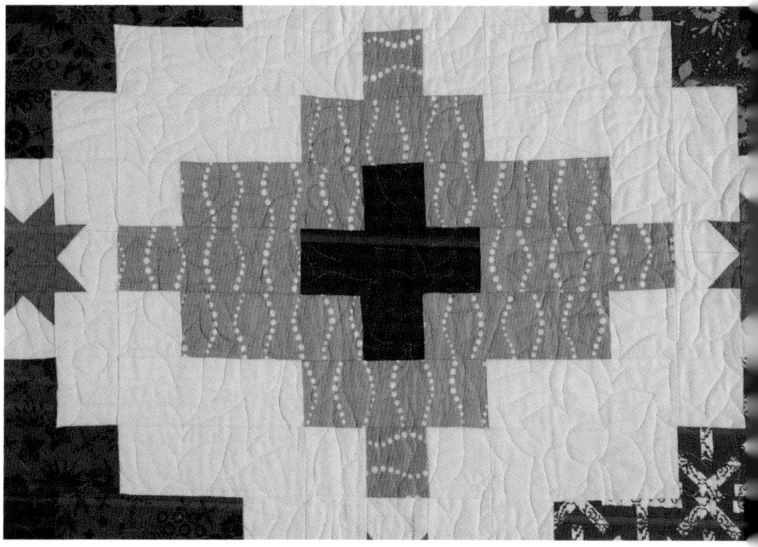

SIDE PARTIAL BLOCKS

To make the side partial blocks, you will need to create the following units for each of the 8 blocks:

- 1 colored 2½" × 4½" rectangle
- 1 white 2½" × 6½" rectangle

[Make 2]

- 1 red 2½" square
- 1 colored 2½" × 6½" rectangle
- 1 white 2½" square

[Make 2]

- 1 red 2½" × 4½" rectangle
- 1 colored 2½" × 6½" rectangle

[Make 1]

5 Lay the units out as pictured. Sew strips together to complete the block. Repeat to make 8 blocks.

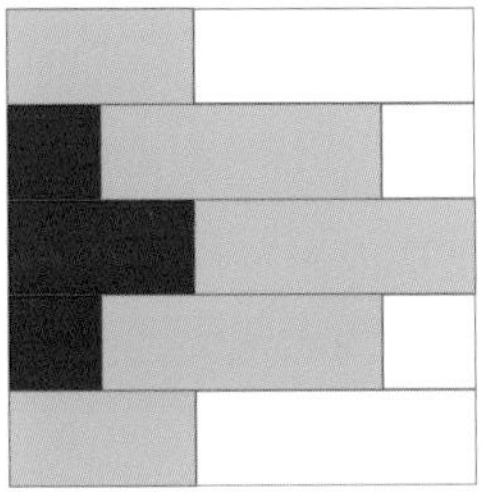

SIDE CONNECTORS

For each side partial block, you will also need to make 2 side connectors, which will be assembled later.

6 Join each of the remaining 2½" colored squares from each of the top and bottom partial blocks with a white 2½" square. Make 16 — 2 per partial block. Set aside.

[Make 16 — 2 per block]

CORNER BLOCKS

To make the 4 corner blocks you will need to create the following units:

- 1 - red 2½" × 4½" rectangle
- 1 - colored 2½" × 6½" rectangle

[Make 1 per corner block]

- 1 — red 2½" square
- 1 — colored 2½" × 6½" rectangle
- 1 — white 2½" square

[Make 1 per corner block]

- 1 — colored 2½" × 4½" rectangle
- 1 — white 2½" × 6½" rectangle

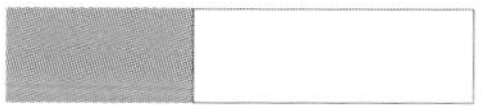

[Make 1 per corner block]

7 Using the corner block segments, assemble 2 corner blocks with the red on the right side of the block and 2 with the red on the left side.

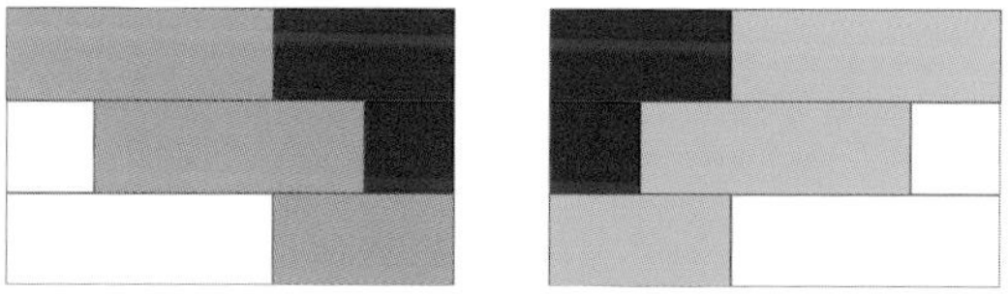

[Make 2 of each corner block, 4 total. Each will be a different color.]

SIDE CONNECTORS FOR CORNER BLOCKS

For each corner block, you will also need to make 1 side connector, which will be assembled later.

Join each of the remaining 2½" colored squares from each of the top and bottom partial blocks with a white 2½" square. Make 4 — 1 per corner block. Set aside.

[Make 4 — 1 per block]

BLUE STAR BLOCKS

8 Draw a diagonal line connecting opposite corners on the back of each of the blue 1½" squares. With right sides together, place a blue 1½" square on the corner of a white 2½" square. Sew on the line drawn on the back of the blue square. Trim the seam to ¼" and press to the blue square. Add a second blue 1½" square to the white square and sew on the drawn line. Trim and press to the blue square. Repeat to make a total of 124 units.

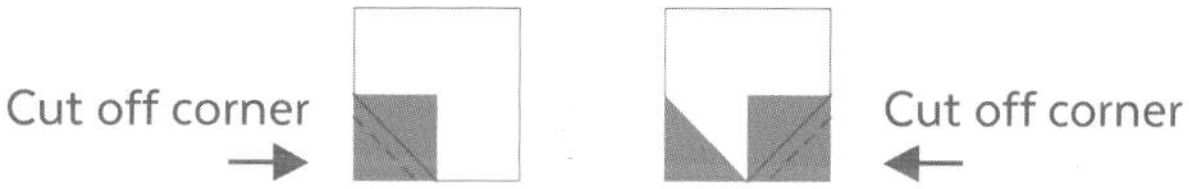

[Make 124 star point units]

9 Using 4 of the star point units, 4 white 2½" squares and 1 blue 2½" square, assemble 31 star blocks. Attach 2 star point squares to opposite sides of the center 2½" blue square. Press to the center blue square. Attach a white 2½" square to opposite sides of 2 additional star point squares. Press to the white outer squares. Assemble the star block by adding the unit with 2 white squares to opposite sides of the center blue square unit.

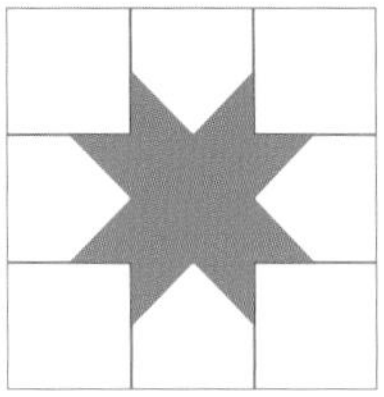

[Make 31 star blocks]

ADDITIONAL TOP AND BOTTOM CONNECTOR UNITS

10 Sew 2 white 2½" × 6½" rectangles together on the long sides. Press. Make 8 sets. Set aside.

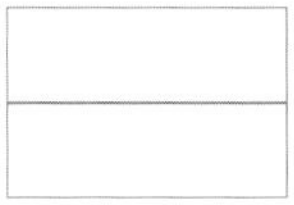

[Make 8]

ADDITIONAL SIDE CONNECTOR UNITS

11 Sew 3 white 2½" × 4½" rectangles together on the long sides. Press. Make 10 sets. Set aside.

[Make 10]

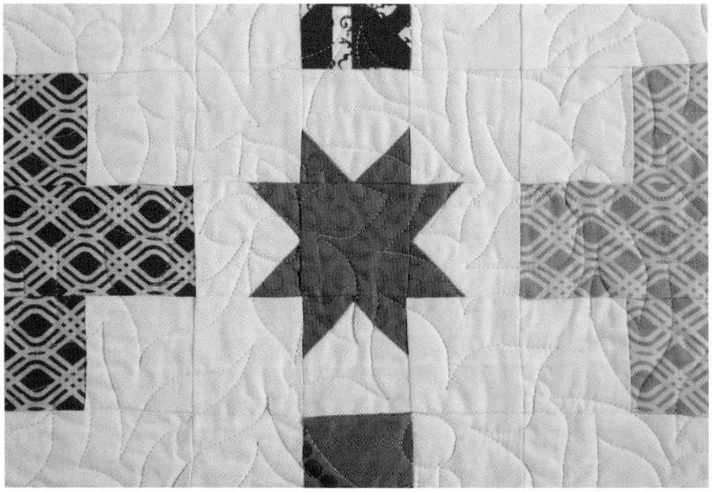

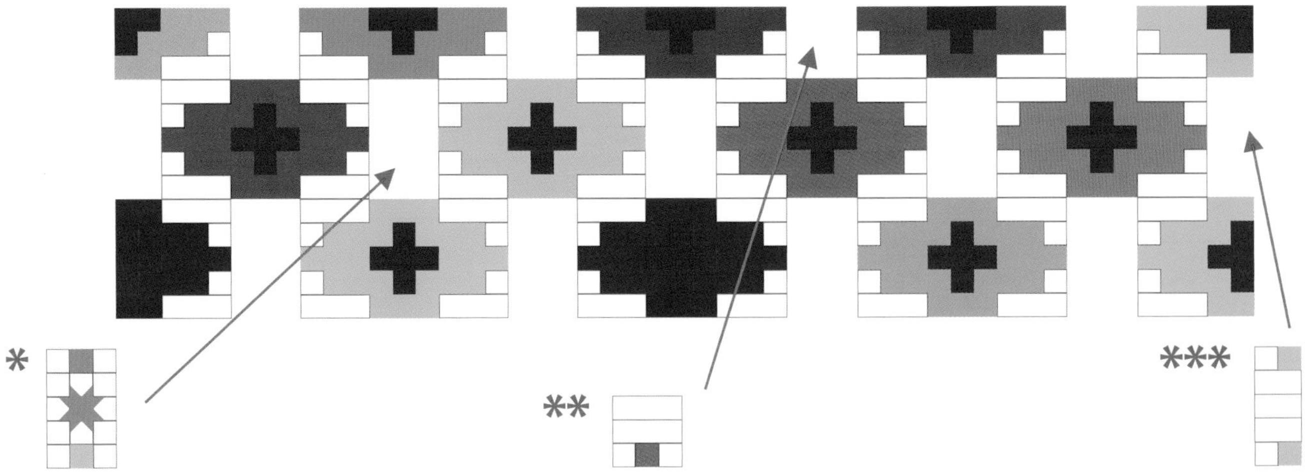

CONNECTOR UNIT ASSEMBLY

Lay out the May Flower blocks, 4 corner blocks, the upper and bottom partial blocks and the side partial blocks on your design wall as shown in the diagram. Check to make sure the color distribution is pleasing and balanced. To complete the pattern, you will need to create the following connector units.

*STAR CONNECTOR BLOCKS

The Star Connector Blocks go in the center of the quilt, as shown with an * on the diagram.

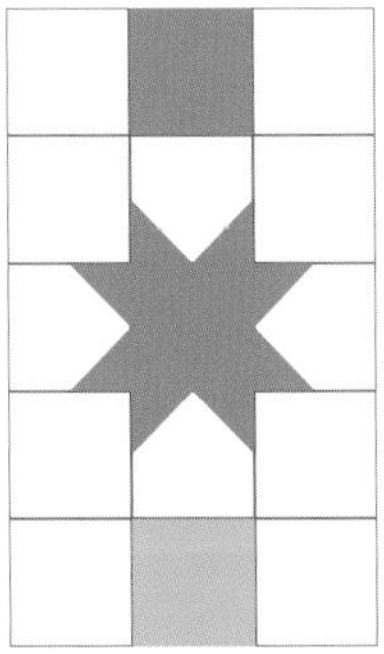

Lay a matching top and bottom connector unit next to the matching print on the May Flower blocks. Place a star block in the center of each. It is important to make sure the connectors match the May Flower blocks to complete the block. Pay close attention when sewing the units together so that the colors don't get mixed up.

Sew each set of star connectors together and press. Once each block is sewn, place on the design wall where they belong. Check to make sure the blocks are sewn correctly and the colors match up.

**TOP AND BOTTOM CONNECTORS

The top and bottom connectors are made of the 8 sets of 2 white strips sewn to a top and bottom connector that matches the top and bottom full rows of May Flower blocks as shown with an ** on the diagram.

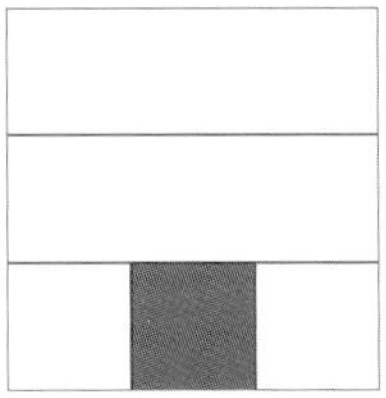

Lay a matching top and bottom connector unit next to the matching print on the May Flower blocks. Place a set of 2 white strips next to it. Pay close attention when sewing the units together so that the colors don't get mixed up.

Sew each together and press. Once each block is sewn, place on the design wall where they belong. Check to make sure the blocks are sewn correctly and the colors match up.

*****SIDE CONNECTORS**

The side connectors are made of the 10 sets of 3 white strips sewn to a side connector unit that matches the side partial blocks shown with an *** on the diagram.

Lay a matching side connector unit next to the matching print on the side partial blocks. Place a set of 3 white strips next to it. Pay close attention when sewing the units together so that the colors don't get mixed up.

Sew each together and press. Once each block is sewn, place on the design wall where they belong. Check to make sure the blocks are sewn correctly and the colors match up.

Quilt Top Assembly

Assemble quilt in rows. Sew rows together to complete the quilt top.

Finishing

Quilting

Layer the backing, batting and top. Quilt as desired. We used an off-white thread and an original quilt design.

Binding

Join the 11 red 2½" × width-of-fabric binding strips on the diagonal and bind the quilt.

Bohemian Rhapsody

Finished Block Size: 6″
Finished Quilt Size: 72½″ × 84½″

Jo is the designer of our duo. Often when she is designing quilts at her computer, her "Sweet Child" Karl is mixing classic rock playlists on the computer next to her. On the day that Jo was working on this quilt, Karl's play list was streaming Queen's 1975 hit "Bohemian Rhapsody." Hearing the song made her think of beautiful bohemian prints. Before we knew it we had named the quilt Bohemian Rhapsody and were on the hunt for the perfect prints to bring the vision to life. Free Spirit fabrics had just what we were looking for. You will notice that the colors are deep, large scale and have very few light colors in them. We think the fabric filled our original vision of the quilt perfectly.

Fabric Requirements

17 — ½ yard cuts of assorted prints

3½ yards Turquoise print

¾ yard Turquoise binding

4½ yards backing

Cutting Instructions

From EACH Print:

Cut 1 — 6⅞" × width-of-fabric strip

- Subcut 5 — 6⅞" squares

Cut 1 — 3½" × width-of-fabric strip

- Subcut 11 — 3½" squares

From Turquoise Print:

Cut 17 — 6⅞" × width-of-fabric strips

- Subcut 84 — 6⅞" squares

From binding:

Cut 8 — 2½" × width-of-fabric strips

Sewing Instructions

Half-Square Triangle Units

1 Draw a diagonal line connecting opposite corners on the back of each of the turquoise 6⅞" squares. Pair each 6⅞" colored square with a 6⅞" turquoise square. With right sides together, sew a ¼" seam on each side of the diagonal line. Cut on the drawn line of each square set. Press to the turquoise print. Repeat to make 168 — 6½" unfinished units.

[**Make 168 — 6½" unfinished turquoise/print half-square triangle units**]

Block

2 Draw a diagonal line connecting opposite corners on the back of each of the colored 3½" squares. Place a colored 3½" square in the corner of the turquoise triangle with right sides together. Sew on the line. Trim the seam to ¼" and press each block to the colored square.

[**Make 168 — 6½" unfinished blocks**]

NOTE: You can save the pieces trimmed off from the corners to make our quilt, Thanks to YOU! on page 102.

Top Assembly

Carefully arrange the blocks as shown in the Quilt Assembly Diagram, twisting and turning to create a 12 × 14 barn-raising layout. Arrange the quilt in rows, then sew the rows together.

Finishing

Quilting
Layer the backing, batting and top. Quilt as desired. We quilted this using a light brown thread and a custom quilting design.

Binding
Join the 8 binding strips on the diagonal and bind the quilt.

[Quilt Assembly Diagram]

Modern Day Patriot

Finished Block Size: 10"
Finished Quilt Size: 88 ½" × 96 ½"

In our family, volunteerism is important to us all. We are active with the local Humane Society, fire department, first responder squad and other community groups. Members of our family have careers in nursing, teaching and translation. Community service in whatever capacity is important to us. Each year we donate a quilt to the firemen's benefit in our local town to raise money for equipment and supplies. We also donate quilts to other worthy causes just like so many quilters around the globe.

We salute all in the world who help in their communities, giving to others and stepping up to help where help is needed. This quilt is for you, the modern day patriot.

Fabric Requirements

4 ½ yards Red solid

2 yards Blue solid

5 yards White solid

7 yards backing

Cutting Instructions

From Red solid:

Cut 27 — 2 ½" × width-of-fabric strips

- 10 strips will be used in the binding
- The remaining strips will be used in block construction

Cut 20 — 2" × width-of-fabric strips

- Subcut 13 strips into 140 — 2" × 3 ½" rectangles
- Subcut 7 strips into 140 — 2" squares

Cut 10 — 4 ½" × width-of-fabric strips to be used for the border

From Blue solid:

Cut 4 — 4 ½" × width-of-fabric strips to be used in block construction

Cut 4 — 6 ½" × width-of-fabric strips

- Subcut into 24 — 6 ½" squares

Cut 9 — 2 ½" × width-of-fabric strips to be used in the border

From White Solid:

Cut 10 — 1 ½" × width-of-fabric strips to be used in the border

Cut 14 — 2" × width-of-fabric strips

- Subcut into 280 — 2" squares

Cut 24 — 2 ½" × width-of-fabric strips

- Subcut 4 strips into 20 — 2 ½" × 6 ½" rectangles
- Subcut 2 strips into 4 — 2 ½" × 10 ½" rectangles
- The remaining strips will be used in block construction

Cut 4 — 3 ½" × width-of-fabric strips

- Subcut into 35 — 3 ½" squares

Cut 12 — 4 ½" × width-of-fabric strips to be used in block construction

Quick Reference Chart

1  30 total units	2  Edge Connector 8 total units	3  Middle Connector 20 total units
4 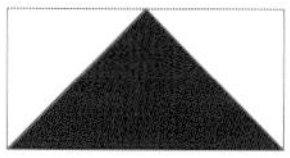 140 total units	5  Star Block 35 total units 6½" unfinished	6  50 total units
7  66 total units	8  Corner Block 4 total units 10½" unfinished	9  Edge Block 16 total units 10½" unfinished
10  Center Block 15 total units 10½" unfinished		

Sewing Instructions

Red-and-Blue Connectors

1 With right sides together, join a red 2½" × width-of-fabric strip to a blue 4½" × width-of-fabric strip along the long sides. Press to the red. With right sides together, sew a second blue 4½" × width-of-fabric strip to the opposite side of the red strip. Press to the red. Make 2 strip sets total. Cut into a total of 30 — 2½" segments.

[Make 30 red-and-blue connectors]

8½" Red-and-White Edge Connectors

2 With right sides together, join a red 2½" × width-of-fabric strip and a white 2½" × width-of-fabric strip along the long sides. Press to the red. Attach a 4½" × width-of-fabric strip to the red strip. Press to the red. Make a total of 2 strip sets. Cut into a total of 8 — 6½" segments.

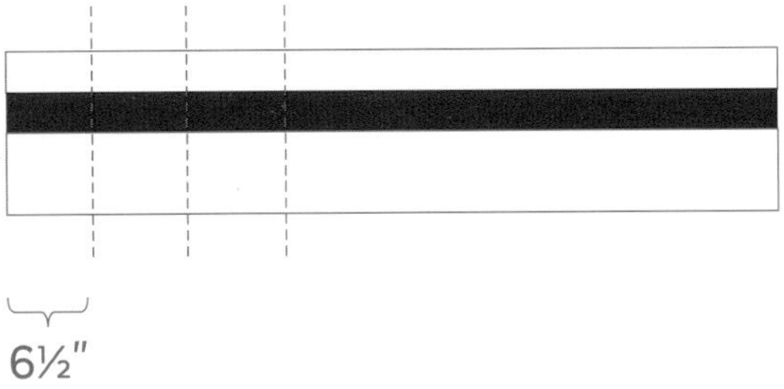

[Make 8 red-and-white connectors]

6½" Red-and-White Middle Connectors

3 With right sides together, join a red 2½" × width-of-fabric strip to a white 2½" × width-of-fabric strip along the long sides. Press to the red. Join a second white 2½" × width-of-fabric strip to the red strip. Press to the red. Make a total of 4 strip sets. Cut into 20 — 6½" segments.

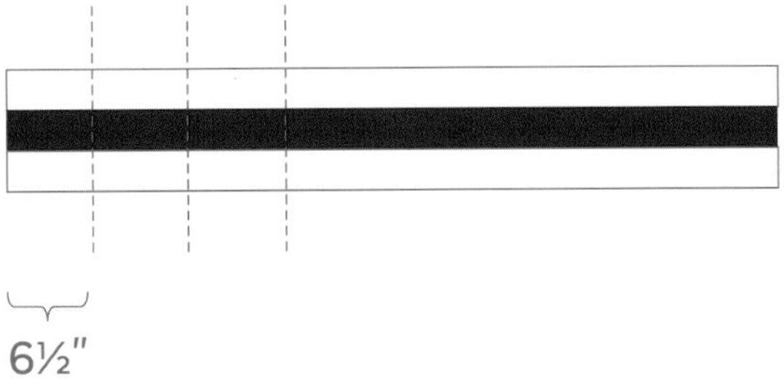

[Make 20]

Flying Geese Units

4 Draw a diagonal line connecting opposite corners on the back of each of the 280 — 2" white squares. Place a white 2" square on the end of a red 2" × 3½" rectangle and sew on the line drawn on the 2" square. Trim the seam to ¼" and press to the white square. Place a second white 2" square on the opposite end of the red rectangle. Sew on the line drawn on the 2" square. Trim the seam to ¼" and press to the white square. Repeat to make 140 red-and-white flying geese units.

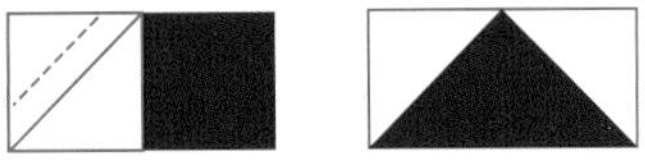

[Make 140 flying geese units]

Star Block

5 Using 4 flying geese units, 4 red 2" squares and 1 white 3½" square, construct 35 stars. Attach 2 flying geese units to opposite sides of the white 3½" square. Press seams to the white square. Attach a red 2" square to the opposite sides of 2 additional flying geese blocks, pressing to the red squares. Sew the rows together to create the star.

[Make 35 — 6½" star blocks]

Short Star Borders

6 With right sides together, join 1 red 2½" × width-of-fabric strip to 1 white 2½" × width-of-fabric strip on the long side. Press to the red. Add a second white 2½" × width-of-fabric strip to the opposite side of the red fabric. Again, press to the red. Make 4 strip sets. Cut into 50 — 2½" segments.

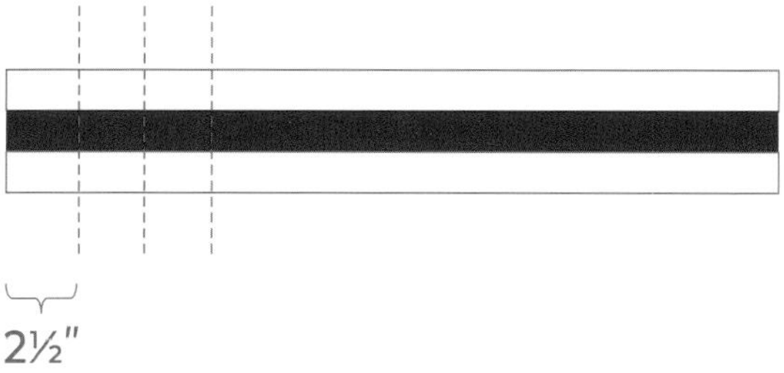

[Make 50]

Long Star Borders

7 With right sides together, join 1 white 4½" × width-of-fabric strip to 1 red 2½" × width-of-fabric strip on the long side. Press to the red. Join a second white 4½" × width-of-fabric strip to the red strip. Press to the red. Make 5 strip sets and cut into 66 — 2½" segments.

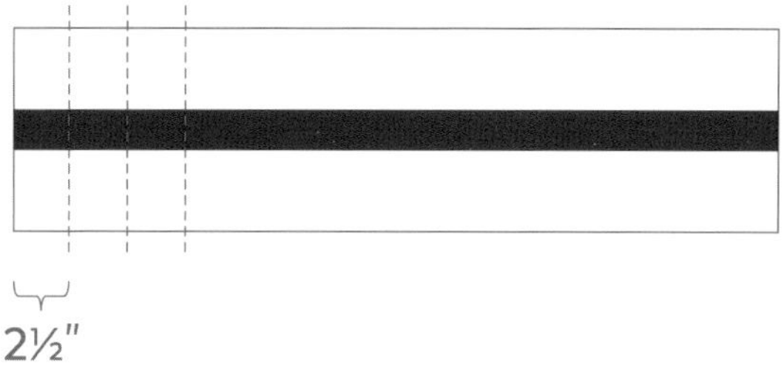

[Make 66]

Corner Blocks

8 Sew 1 — 2½" × 6½" pieced unit and a 2½" × 6½" white rectangle to opposite sides of a star block. Press away from the star. Add 1 — 2½" × 10½" pieced unit to one side and a 2½" × 10½" white rectangle to the opposite side. Press away from the star. Create 4 corner blocks.

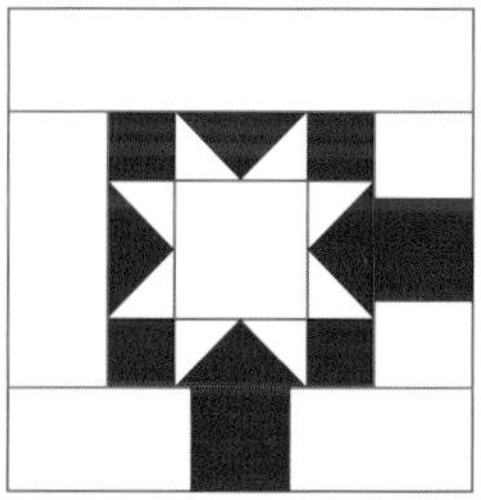

[Make 4 — 10½" unfinished corner blocks]

Edge Blocks

9 Attach a pieced 2½" × 6½" unit and a white 2½" × 6½" rectangle to opposite sides of a star block. Press the side segments away from the star. Stitch a 2½" × 10½" pieced unit to the opposite sides of the star. Press away from the star. Make a total of 16 blocks. These blocks will be used to create the outer columns of blocks as well as the top and bottom of the middle columns.

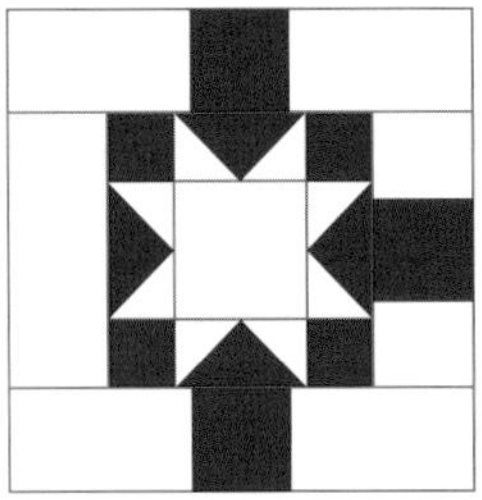

[Make 16 — 10½" unfinished edge blocks]

Center Blocks

10 To make the inner blocks, attach 2 — 2½" × 6½" pieced units to opposite sides of the star block. Press away from the star. Attach 2 — 2½" × 10½" segments to the remaining opposite sides of the block. Press away from the star. Make a total of 15 blocks. These blocks will be used in the center of the quilt.

[Make 15 — 10½" unfinished center blocks]

Top Assembly

This quilt is assembled in a column format.

Side Columns
Using 2 corner blocks, 5 edge blocks, and 6 red-and-blue connectors, make 2 side columns.

[Make 2]

Sashing Columns
Using 2 – 8½" red-and-white connectors, 5 – 6½" red-and-white connectors, and 6 blue 6½" squares, assemble 4 columns.

[Make 4]

Center Columns
Using 2 edge blocks, 5 center blocks and 6 red-and-blue connectors, make 3 middle columns.

[Make 3]

Join the 9 columns as shown in the assembly diagram. Press.

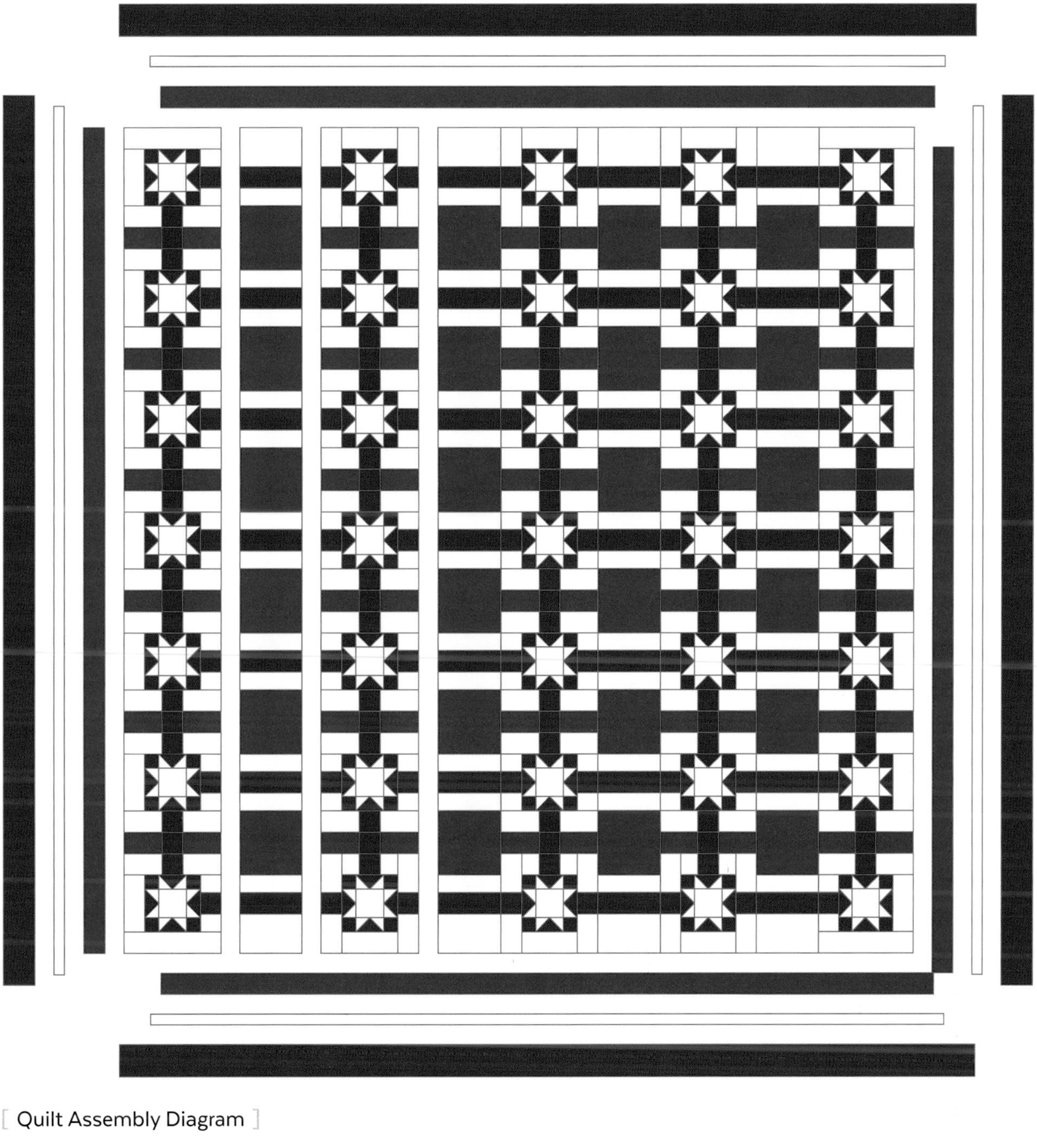

[Quilt Assembly Diagram]

Borders

Join 9 — 2½" × width-of-fabric blue strips on the diagonal. Press. Measure the quilt vertically through the middle. Cut 2 pieces of the blue 2½" strip to this measurement. Attach to the sides of the quilt and press to the blue border. Measure the quilt horizontally through the middle. Cut 2 pieces of the blue 2½" strip to this measurement. Connect to the top and bottom edges of the quilt. Press to the blue.

Join the 10 white 1½" × width-of-fabric strips on the diagonal. Press. Measure the quilt vertically through the middle. Cut 2 pieces of the white 1½" strip to this measurement. Attach to the sides of the quilt and press to the white border. Measure the quilt horizontally through the middle. Cut 2 pieces of the white 1½" strip to this measurement. Connect to the top and bottom edges of the quilt. Press to the white.

Join the 10 red 4½" × width-of-fabric strips. Press. Measure the quilt vertically through the middle. Cut 2 pieces of the red 4½" strip to this measurement. Attach to the sides of the quilt and press to the red border. Measure the quilt horizontally through the middle. Cut 2 pieces of the red 4½" strip to this measurement. Connect to the top and bottom edges of the quilt. Press to the red.

Finishing

Quilting

Layer the backing, batting and top. Quilt as desired. We used white thread and a design from The Pajama Quilter (see resources page 112).

Binding

Join the 10 red binding strips on the diagonal and bind the quilt.

Puddle Duck

Finished Block Size: 20"
Finished Quilt Size: 72½" × 72½"

When we get stuck, we often call for help from our blog readers, asking them for cleaning tips, good books to read or quilt naming help. On this quilt we were stuck. We loved the big oversized blocks. We loved the diagonal created by the yellow in the center of the blocks. We loved the quilt, but could not come up with a name. Finally we put up a blog post pleading for help. We laid the fabric out and asked for suggestions. One reader suggested Puddle Duck and that was it — the name was perfect! After her suggestion, we could see that the yellow looks like ducks playing in a puddle of water.

Fabric Requirements

4 ½ yards Neutral background

¾ yard Yellow print

1 yard Green print

4 — ½-yard cuts of Blue print

½ yard Pink print

¾ yard Green binding

4 yards backing

Cutting Instructions

From Neutral background:

Cut 6 — 6 ½" × width-of-fabric strips

- Subcut 36 — 6 ½" squares

Cut 7 — 6 ½" × width-of-fabric strips to be used in the border

Cut 23 — 2 ½" × width-of-fabric strips

- Subcut 5 strips into 72 — 2 ½" squares
- Subcut 18 strips into 144 — 2 ½" × 4 ½" rectangles

Cut 2 — 4 ½" × width-of-fabric strips

- Subcut 9 — 4 ½" squares

From Yellow fabric:

Cut 3 — 5 ¼" × width-of-fabric strips

- Subcut 18 — 5 ¼" squares

Cut 3 — 2 ½" × width-of-fabric strips

- Subcut 36 — 2 ½" squares

From Green fabric:

Cut 2 — 5 ¼" × width-of-fabric strips

- Subcut 8 — 5 ¼" squares

Cut 8 — 2 ½" × width-of-fabric strips

- Subcut 128 — 2 ½" squares

From Each Blue and Pink fabric:

Cut 1 — 5 ¼" × width-of-fabric strip

- Subcut into 2 — 5 ¼" squares

Cut 2 — 2 ½" × width-of-fabric strips

- Subcut into 32 — 2 ½" squares

From binding fabric:

Cut 8 — 2 ½" × width-of-fabric strips

[Quick Reference Chart]

1  2½" × 4½" unfinished 16 per block	2 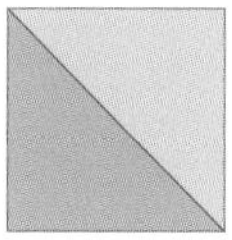 4 per block	3  4½" unfinished 4 per block
4 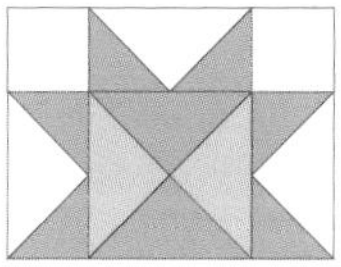 Star Unit 1 2 per block	5 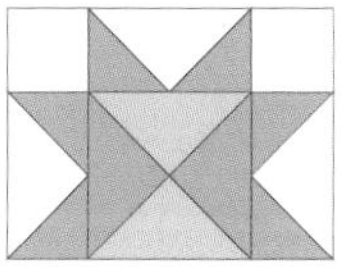 Star Unit 2 2 per block	6 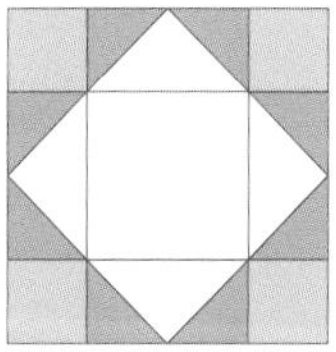 Center Unit 1 per block
7  20½" unfinished 4 blue, 4 green and 1 pink		

Sewing Instructions

To make one block, you will need:

4 white 6½" squares

8 white 2½" squares

16 white 2½" × 4½" rectangles

1 white 4½" square

2 yellow 5¼" squares

4 yellow 2½" squares

32 colored (same print — green, blue or pink) 2½" squares

2 colored (same print — green, blue or pink) 5¼" squares

Flying Geese Units

1 Draw a diagonal line connecting opposite corners on the back of the small colored squares. Place 1 colored 2½" square on a corner of a 2½" × 4½" white rectangle. With right sides together, sew diagonally on the line drawn on the colored square. Trim the seam to ¼" and press to the colored square. Repeat for the opposite side. Repeat to make 16 flying geese units for each block.

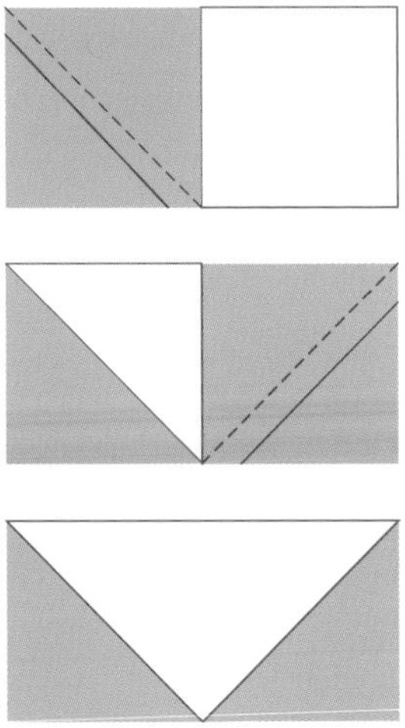

[Make 16 flying geese units]

TIP: Save the trimmed corners to make Thanks to YOU!! on page 102.

Quarter-Square Triangle Units

2-3 Draw a diagonal line connecting opposite corners on the back of 2 yellow 5¼" squares. With right sides together, pair with a colored 5¼" colored square. Sew ¼" on each side of the drawn line. Cut on the drawn line and press to the colored fabric. Repeat with the remaining yellow square and matching colored square to make 4 half-square triangle units.

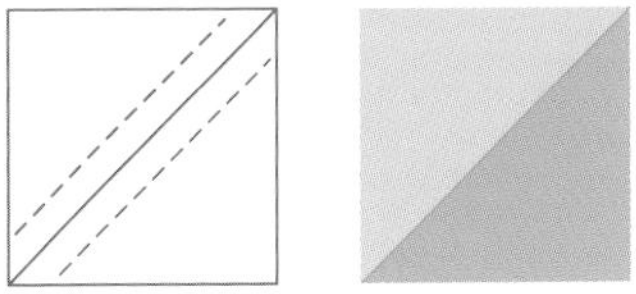

[Make 4 half-square triangle units]

Draw a second diagonal line connecting opposite corners on the back of 2 of the half-square triangles, making sure to draw over the seam, not along it. Match a second half-square triangle to the first, matching opposite colors. Sew a seam ¼" from each side of the drawn line. Cut on the line and press. Make 4 — 4½" quarter-square triangle units.

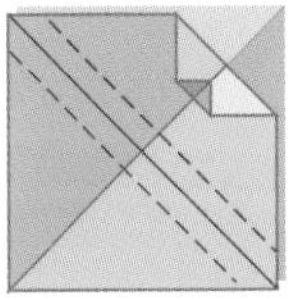

[Make 4 — 4½" quarter-square triangle units]

NOTE: Star unit 1 and star unit 2 look very similar, but it is important to make sure the quarter-square triangle units in the center are turned correctly to make the block work.

Star Unit 1

4 Assemble star unit 1 as shown, attaching 2 flying geese blocks to the opposite sides of the quarter-square triangle to match up with the yellow triangles. Press to the flying geese unit. Attach a 2½" square to each end of another flying geese unit. Press to the white square. Attach the quarter-square triangle unit to the 2 flying geese units. Press to the flying geese unit with the squares attached. Make 2.

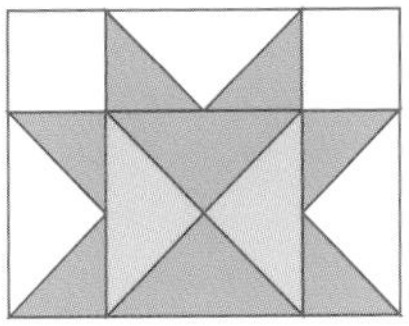

[Make 2 Star Unit 1]

Star Unit 2

5 To complete star unit 2, attach flying geese units to the opposite sides of the quarter-square triangle on the colored side. Press to the flying geese. With right sides together, attach a white 2½" square to the opposite ends of one of the remaining flying geese units. Press to the white squares. Attach the flying geese unit to one of the yellow quarter-square triangle sides. Press to the flying geese segment. Repeat with 3 of the remaining flying geese units and quarter-square triangle.

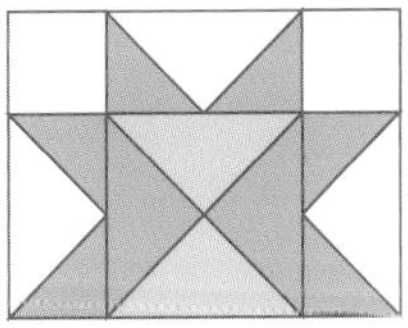

[Make 2 Star Unit 2]

Center Unit

6 Attach 2 of the 4 remaining flying geese units to opposite sides of the white 4½" square. Press to the flying geese. Attach a yellow 2½" square to each end of the remaining flying geese. Press to the yellow. Attach these units to the opposite sides of the white square.

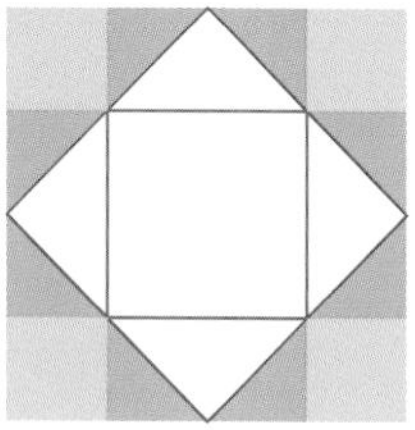

[Make 1 center unit]

Block Assembly

7 Attach 2 white 6½" squares to opposite sides of a star unit 1 block. Press to the white square. Repeat to make a second matching unit.

Sew 2 star unit 2 blocks to each side of the center unit. Press.

Assemble the block as shown. Make 4 green, 4 blue and 1 pink block.

[Make 4 green, 4 blue and 1 pink block. Each block is 20½" unfinished.]

Top Assembly

Assemble the blocks in a 3 × 3 layout with the blue blocks in the corners, green blocks forming a cross, and the pink block in the center.

Borders

Join the 7 — 6½" × width-of-fabric strips end to end. Press. Measure your quilt vertically through the middle. Cut 2 — 6½" strips to this length. Attach to the sides of the quilt. Press to the border. Measure your quilt horizontally through the middle. Cut 2 — 6½" strips to this length. Attach to the top and bottom of the quilt. Press to the border.

Finishing

Quilting

Layer the backing, batting and top and quilt as desired. We used an off-white thread and a custom quilt design.

Binding

Join the 8 green binding strips on the diagonal and bind.

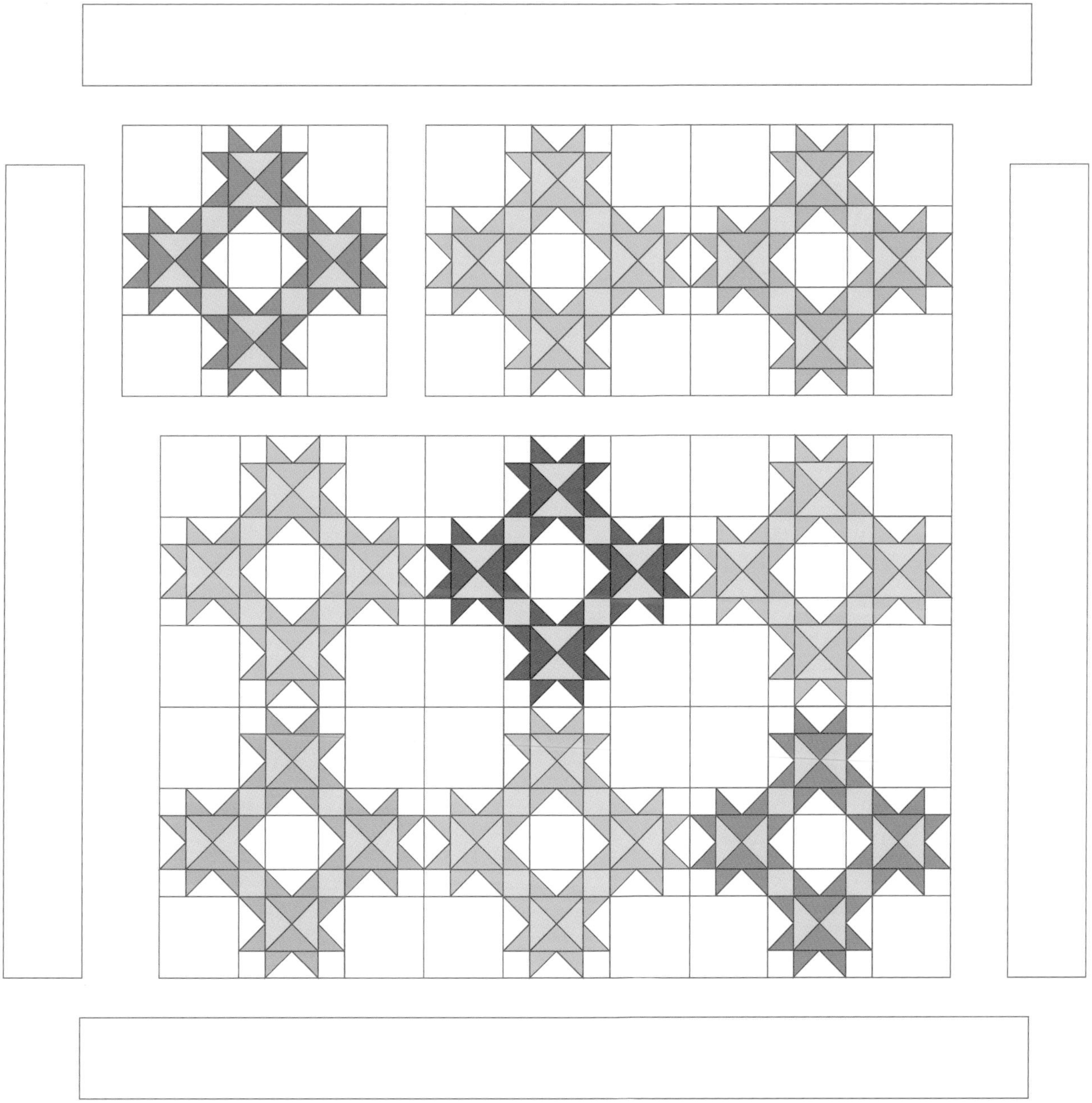

[Quilt Assembly Diagram]

Modalicious

Finished Block Size:
3½" × 3½"
Finished Quilt Size:
82½" × 94½"

At an auction we bought an old quilt book from back in the 80s. While paging through it, we found blocks that we hadn't seen before. Curiosity got the better of us and before long we found ourselves sitting at the computer, playing with the design and coloring. Because all the blocks in the book were in black and white, color placement became even more fun and a new design emerged. Quilts come to life first on paper and eventually, if we really like them, they come to life in fabric. Moda Fabrics has been so good to us while we worked on this book. We decided to use all sorts of delicious Moda Fabrics in this project and to call it Modalicious.

Fabric Requirements

7 yards White

1 yard Red

¾ yard Red binding

1 yard EACH of assorted scraps, at least 3½" wide in Yellow, Purple, Orange, Pink, Blue and Green.

6 yards backing

Additional Supplies

Tri-Recs Tools acrylic ruler or template-making supplies

Cutting Instructions

From White fabric:

Cut 27 — 2" × width-of-fabric strips

- Subcut 18 strips into 346 — 2" squares. The remaining strips will be used in the border.

Cut 51 — 3½" × width-of-fabric strips

- Using the side triangles of the Tri-Recs Tools or Templates B and C found on page 82, cut 1,408 triangles making sure half are left-oriented and half are right-oriented.

From Red fabric:

Cut 9 — 2½" × width-of-fabric strips for binding

Cut 16 — 2" × width-of-fabric strips

- Subcut into 173 — 2" × 3½" rectangles

[Quick Reference Chart]

1	2	3
		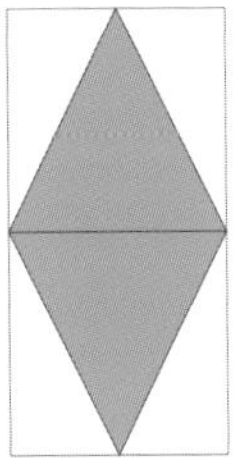
173 total	116 yellow 118 purple 118 orange 118 pink 117 blue 118 green	55 of each color

NOTE: Make sure there are at least 2 matching triangles per print when cutting the colored triangles.

From scraps:

Using the large triangle of the Tri-Recs Tool or Template A on page 82, cut the following:

- 116 Yellow triangles
- 118 Purple triangles
- 118 Orange triangles
- 118 Pink triangles
- 117 Blue triangles
- 118 Green triangles

Sewing Instructions

FLYING GEESE UNITS

1 Draw a diagonal line connecting opposite corners on the back of each white 2" square. With right sides together, place a white 2" square on one end of the red 2" × 3½" rectangle. Sew on the line drawn on the 2" square. Trim the seam to ¼" and press to the white square. Place a second white square on the opposite end of the rectangle. Sew on the drawn line. Trim the seam to ¼" and press to the white square. Repeat to make 173 flying geese units.

[Make 173 flying geese units]

TRIANGLE UNITS

2 Join a white right-oriented triangle with a colored triangle. Press to the colored triangle. Join a white left-oriented triangle with one of the colored triangles. Press to the white triangle. Make 116 yellow, 118 pink, 117 blue, 118 purple, 118 orange and 118 green triangle units. Set aside 6 yellow, 8 purple, 8 orange, 8 pink, 8 green, and 7 blue units.

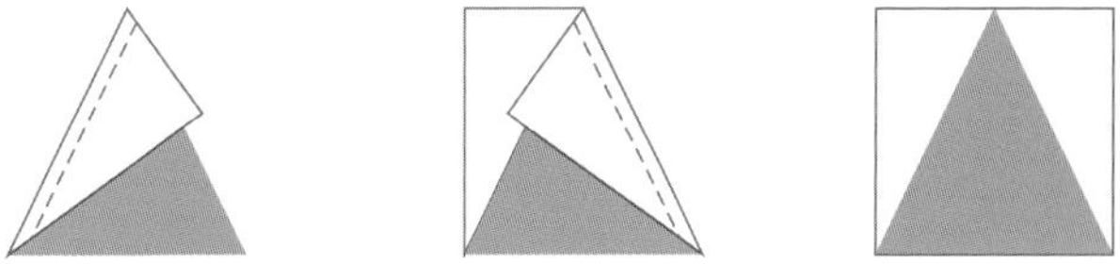

[Make 116 yellow, 118 pink, 117 blue, 118 purple, 118 orange and 118 green triangle units]

DIAMOND UNITS

3 With right sides together, join two identical print triangles along the wider colored base to make a diamond. Press. Repeat with each color to make 55 diamonds in each color.

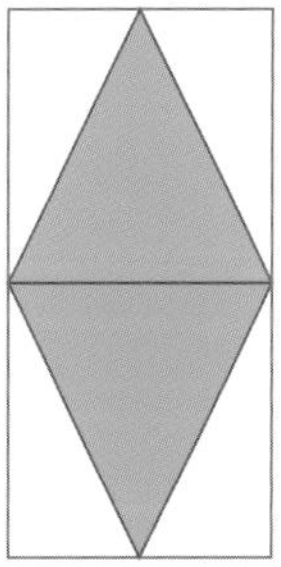

[Make 55 diamonds of each color]

BASES AND POINTS

From the single triangles that were set aside, leave 3 yellow, 4 purple, 4 orange, 4 pink, 4 green and 3 blue whole. The remaining triangles will be cut into either bases or points.

Bases

To trim to a base, measure 2" from the base of the triangle and cut with a rotary cutter as shown. Cut 1 yellow, 2 purple, 2 orange, 2 pink, 2 green and 2 blue bases.

Points

To trim to a point, measure 2" from the point of the triangle and cut with a rotary color as shown. Cut 2 yellow, 2 purple, 2 orange, 2 pink, 2 green and 2 blue points.

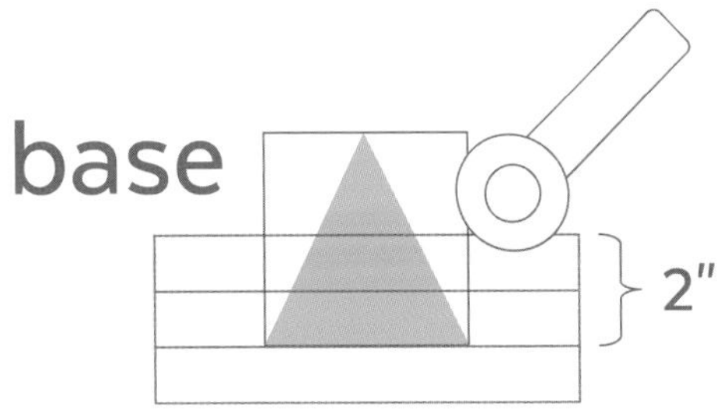

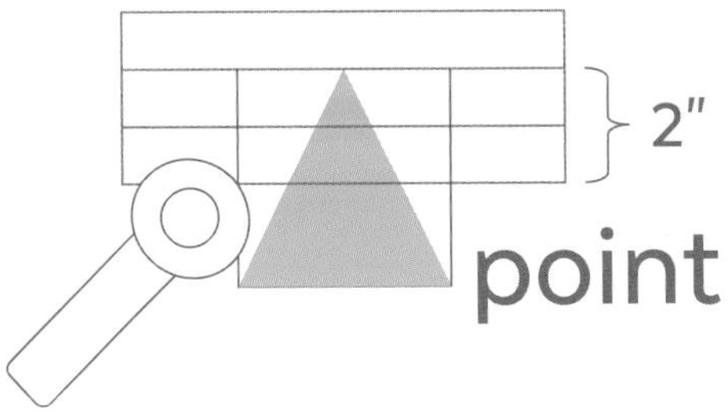

Top Assembly

Assemble the quilt top as shown in the quilt assembly diagram. Note that this quilt is assembled in columns. You will need to take special care to assemble each column correctly. Once you have assembled each column, join them together to create the diagonal pattern of the quilt. Press.

Borders

Join the 9 white 2″ × width-of-fabric strips on the diagonal. Press.

Measure the quilt vertically through the middle. Cut 2 pieces of the solid white border to this measurement. Attach these 2 pieces to the sides of the quilt. Press to the white 2″ border. Measure the quilt horizontally through the middle. Cut 2 pieces of the white border to this measurement. Attach to the top and bottom of the quilt. Press to the white 2″ border.

Finishing

Quilting

Layer the backing, batting and top. Quilt as desired. We used an allover design with a white thread.

Binding

Join the 9 – 2½″ × width-of-fabric red binding strips together on the diagonal and bind.

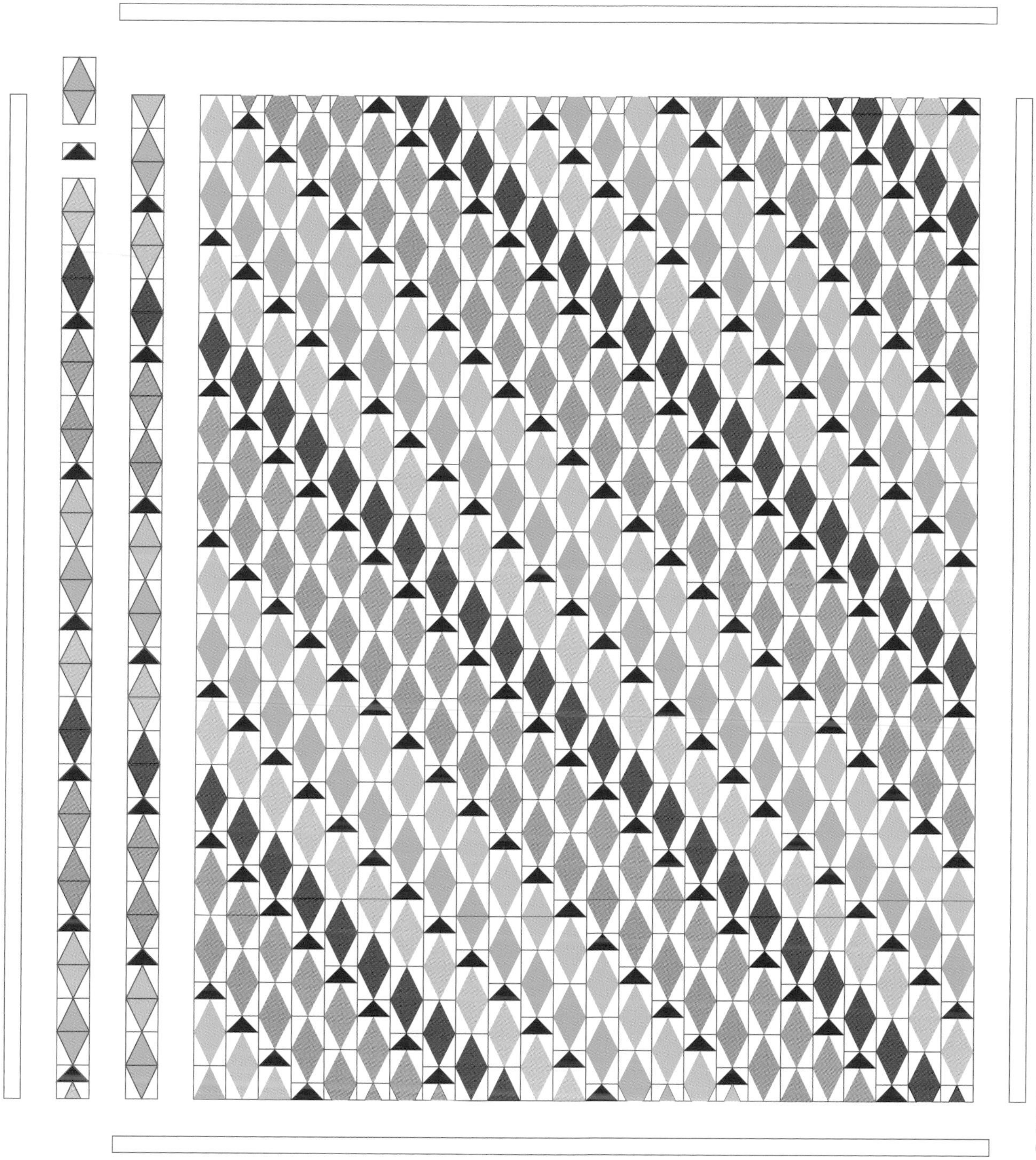

[Quilt Assembly Diagram]

[Template A]

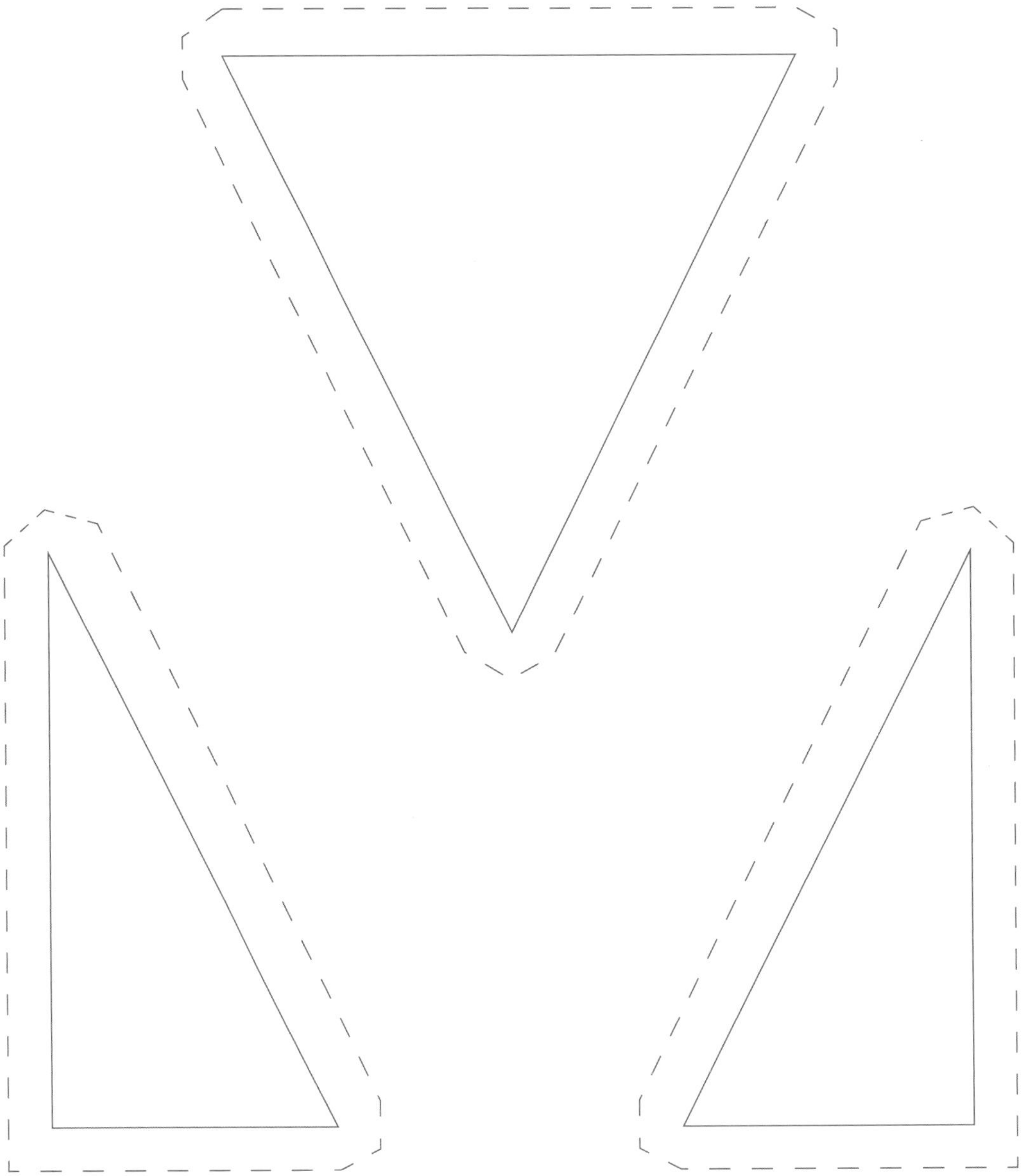

[Template B]

[Template C]

1 inch

Pilot Knob

Finished Block Size: 6"
Finished Quilt Size: 72½" × 94½"

In the early 1900s, two sisters immigrated to the United States from Sweden. Once here, they reunited with two brothers from the old country and each sister married one of the brothers. One couple settled in Pocahontas County, Iowa, and the other in Waseca County, Minnesota. To this day, each year in August the families get together in the middle spot — Pilot Knob State Park, near Forest City, Iowa. We are descendants of the Minnesota couple. At the park, trails and paths wind up and down, leading to a stone tower that visitors can climb to enjoy the view. In 2012, the tower at Pilot Knob State Park became even more special as Jo's son proposed there to the woman who is now his wife.

We designed this quilt as the perfect one to bring to our family picnic and to yours too!

Fabric Requirements

½ yard Turquoise print

½ yard Red print

½ yard Yellow print

½ yard Gray print

1½ yards Dark Blue print

1½ yards Light Blue print

1½ yards Red Stripe print

1½ yards Red Check print

1¾ yards White print

¾ yard Red print binding

6 yards backing

Cutting Instructions

From Turquoise (for centers):

Cut 6 — 2½" × width-of-fabric strips

- Subcut 3 strips into 35 — 2½" squares
- The remaining strips will be used in the construction of the sashing.

From Red (for centers):

Cut 6 — 2½" × width-of-fabric strips

- Subcut 3 strips into 47 — 2½" squares
- The remaining strips will be used in the construction of the sashing.

From Yellow (for centers):

Cut 6 — 2½" × width-of-fabric strips

- Subcut 3 strips into 34 — 2½" squares
- The remaining strips will be used in the construction of the sashing.

From Gray (for centers):

Cut 4 — 2½" × width-of-fabric strips

- Subcut 2 strips into 23 — 2½" squares
- The remaining strips will be used in the construction of the sashing.

From Dark Blue print:
Cut 17 — 2½" × width-of-fabric strips

- Subcut 12 strips into 70 — 2½" × 6½" rectangles, 66 to be used in block construction, 4 to be used in quilt assembly
- Subcut 5 strips into 68 — 2½" squares

From Light Blue print:
Cut 17 — 2½" × width-of-fabric strips

- Subcut 12 strips into 72 — 2½" × 6½" rectangles
- Subcut 5 strips into 72 — 2½" squares

From Red Stripe print:
Cut 17 — 2½" × width-of-fabric strips

- Subcut 12 strips into 71 — 2½" × 6½" rectangles, 65 to be used in block construction, 6 to be used in quilt assembly
- Subcut 5 strips into 66 — 2½" squares

From Red Check print:
Cut 17 — 2½" × width-of-fabric strips

- Subcut 12 strips into 72 — 2½" × 6½" rectangles
- Subcut 5 strips into 72 — 2½" squares

From White print:
Cut 22 — 2½" × width-of-fabric strips

From Red binding print:
Cut 9 — 2½" × width-of-fabric strips

Sewing Instructions

Blocks
With right sides together, sew a 2½" square to each side of the center square. Press to the darker fabric.

Using the 2½" × 6½" rectangles, sew a matching rectangle to the top edge of each unit. Press to the rectangle.

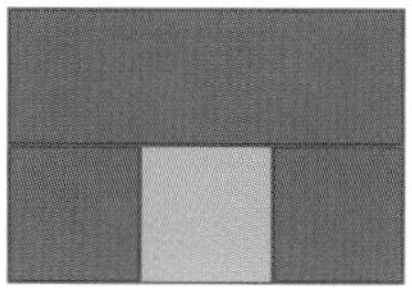

Set aside one dark blue with turquoise center, one dark blue with red center and one red stripe with yellow center. These will be used in the final quilt assembly to create the up and down design at the top and bottom of the columns.

To the remaining units add a matching 2½" × 6½" rectangle to the bottom. Use the chart below to see how many blocks of each color combinations to make.

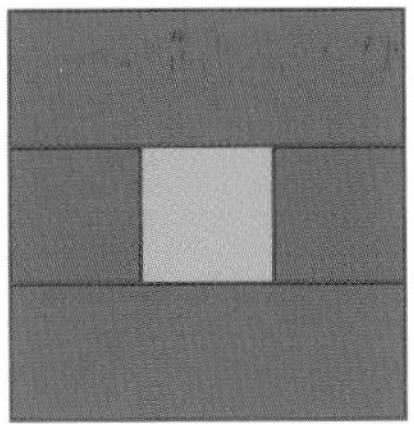

For example you will need to make 9 blocks that have Light Blue around the outside with a turquoise center.

	Turquoise Center	Red Center	Gray Center	Yellow Center
Light Blue Print	9	12	6	9
Dark Blue Print	9	12	5	8
Red Check	9	12	6	9
Red Stripe	8	11	6	8

Sashing

The sashing pieces are made by strip piecing. Join a white 2½" × width-of-fabric strip to each side of the center 2½" × width-of-fabric strip. You will need to make 3 sets with turquoise centers, 3 sets with red centers, 3 sets with yellow centers, and 2 sets with gray centers. Press to the colored strip.

Cut the following 2½" segments from the strip sets:

- From the turquoise, cut 35 segments
- From the red, cut 46 segments
- From the yellow, cut 36 segments
- From the gray, cut 23 segments

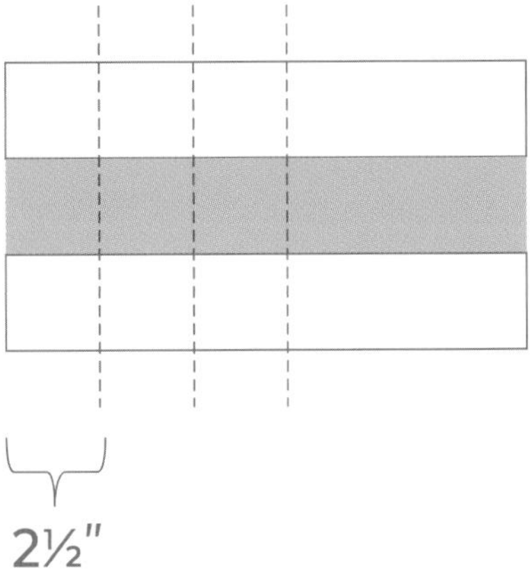

ORGANIZATIONAL TIP: We laid out all of our blocks with the 6½" rectangle running horizontally. This allowed us to match seams every 2" rather than every 6".

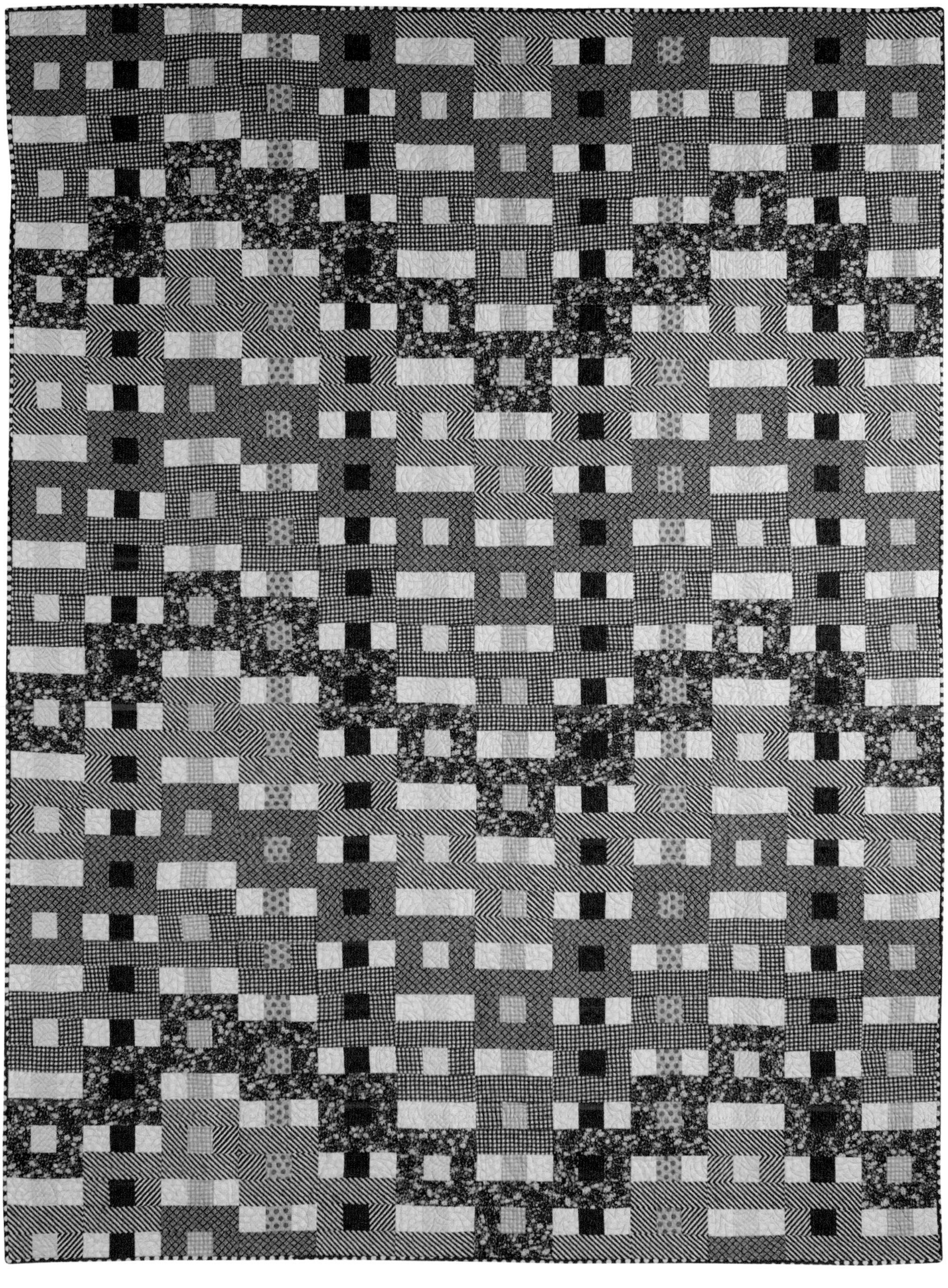

Top Assembly

Assemble the quilt top as shown. Note that this quilt is assembled in columns. You will need to take special care to assemble each column correctly. Once you have assembled each column, join them together to create the up and down pattern of the quilt. Press.

Finishing

Quilting

Layer the backing, batting and top. Quilt as desired. We used a red thread and a quilt design from The Pajama Quilter (See resources page 112).

Binding

Join the binding strips on the diagonal. Press and bind.

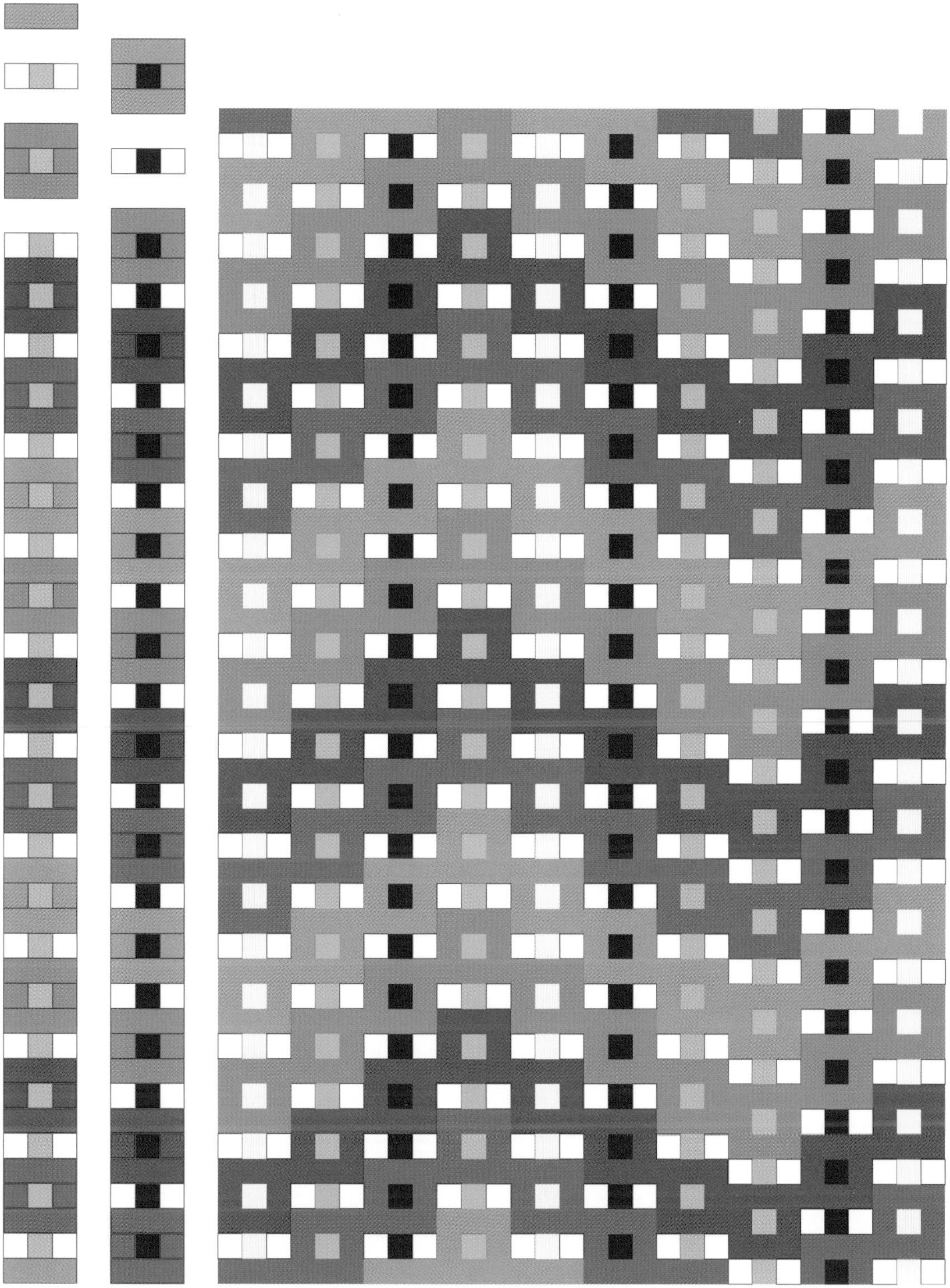

[Quilt Assembly Diagram]

School Bus

Finished Block Size: 9″
Finished Quilt Size: 61½″ × 81½″

It's no secret that we have trouble naming quilts. We are honestly awful at it. So many of our quilt names start by using the name of the fabric line they were made with, or some other silly name that ends in "delight" like Pink Delight or Depot Delight or even after Kelli's beagle, Puppycat, with Puppycat Delight.

So far this quilt has been named Barcelona after the Moda fabric line it was made with, Moonlight Bay after our quilting retreat at Lake Okoboji and Summer Solstice as the blending of the colors reminded us of the longest day of summer. None of those names stuck.

Then after the quilt was finished we showed it to Jo's husband. His typical response is "cool." If he says anything more than "cool," we know the quilt is either really good or really bad. Upon seeing this one he said, "Why, that looks like a big yellow school bus." So the name of this quilt is Barcelona Moonlight Bay Lake Okoboji Summer Solstice School Bus — but we're calling it School Bus for short.

Fabric Requirements

4 ¼ yards Black polka dot

1 yard Yellow solid

½ yard each of 4 Orange prints

¼ yard each of 6 Turquoise prints

½ yard Off-White print

¾ yard striped binding

4 yards backing

Cutting Instructions

From Black:

Cut 10 — 1½" × width-of-fabric strips for the center yellow blocks and border

Cut 10 — 4½" × width-of-fabric strips for the sashing

Cut 10 — 3⅞" × width-of-fabric strips

- Subcut 96 — 3⅞" squares

Cut 3 — 3½" × width-of-fabric strips

- Subcut 24 — 3½" squares

Cut a total of 21 — 2" × width-of-fabric strips for block construction and the border

From Yellow:

Cut 7 — 1½" × width-of-fabric strips for yellow block centers

- Subcut 5 strips into 48 — 1½" × 3½" rectangles
- The remaining strips will be used in the yellow center block construction.

Cut 9 — 2" × width-of-fabric strips for block construction

From EACH of 4 Orange Prints:

Cut 3 — 3⅞" × width-of-fabric strips (total 12)

- Subcut into 96 — 3⅞" squares

From EACH of 6 Turquoise Prints:

Cut 2 — 2" × width-of-fabric strips (total 12)

From White print:

Cut 8 — 1½" × width-of-fabric strips

- Subcut 3 strips into 63 — 1½" squares for the sashing

From Binding fabric:

Cut 8 — 2½" × width-of-fabric strips

[Quick Reference Chart]

1  3½" × 3½" unfinished 4 per block 192 total	2 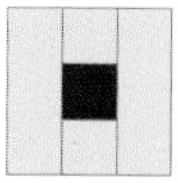 3½" × 3½" unfinished 24 total units	3  3½" × 3½" unfinished 96 total units
4 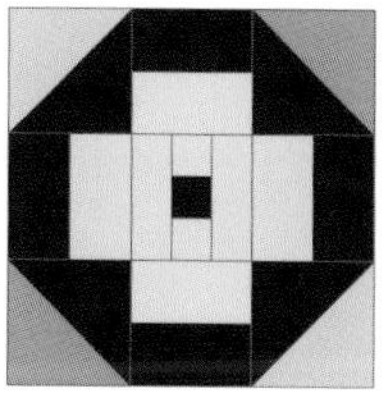 Block A 9½" × 9½" unfinished 24 total units	5  3½" × 3½" unfinished 4 per block 24 sets — 96 total	6  Block B 9½" × 9½" unfinished 24 total units
7  110 units		

Sewing Instructions

BLOCKS

1 Draw a diagonal line connecting opposite corners on the back of each orange square. With right sides together, place a 3⅞" orange square on top of a black 3⅞" square. Sew ¼" seam on each side of the drawn line. Cut on the drawn line and press to the black. Each orange and black set will yield 2 — 3½" half-square triangles. Repeat with each orange and black square to make 192 half-square triangles.

[Make 192 — 3½" unfinished half-square triangle units]

2 To make the yellow block centers, join a yellow 1½" strip to each side of a black 1½" strip. Make 1 strip set. Press each to the black. Cut into a total of 24 — 1½" segments.

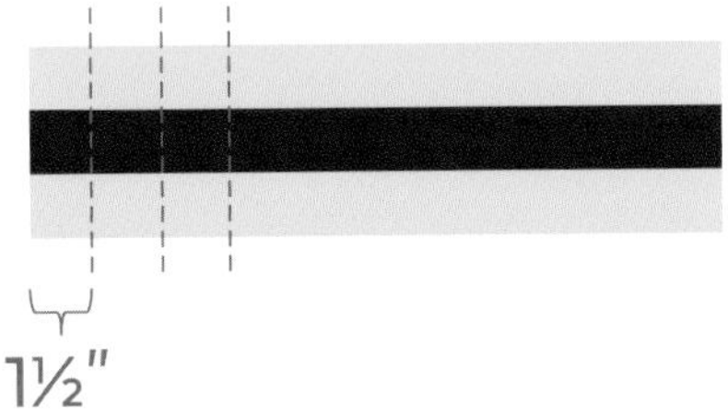

[Make 24 — 1½" segments for yellow block centers]

Sew a 1½" × 3½" yellow rectangle to each side of the strip segment. Press to the yellow.

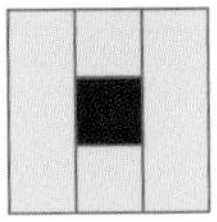

[Make 24 — 3½" unfinished yellow block centers]

3 Sew a 2" black width-of-fabric strip to a 2" yellow width-of-fabric strip. Press to the black fabric. Make 9 strip sets. Subcut each strip set into 3½" segments for a total of 96 — 3½" segments.

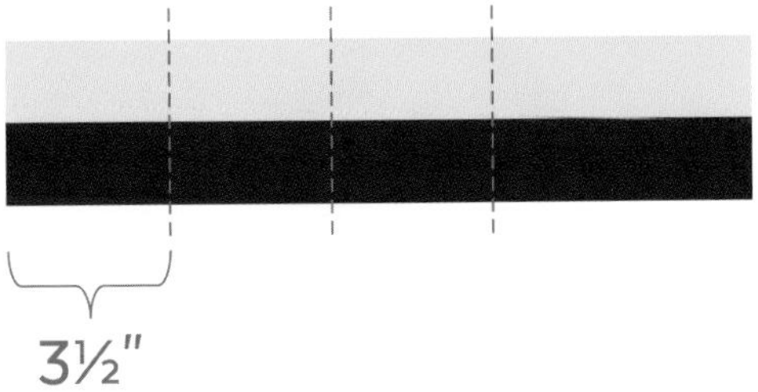

[Make 96 — 3½" segments for yellow blocks]

Block A Assembly

4 Assemble the blocks using 4 random orange and black half-square triangles, 4 yellow and black square segments, and a yellow framed center unit.

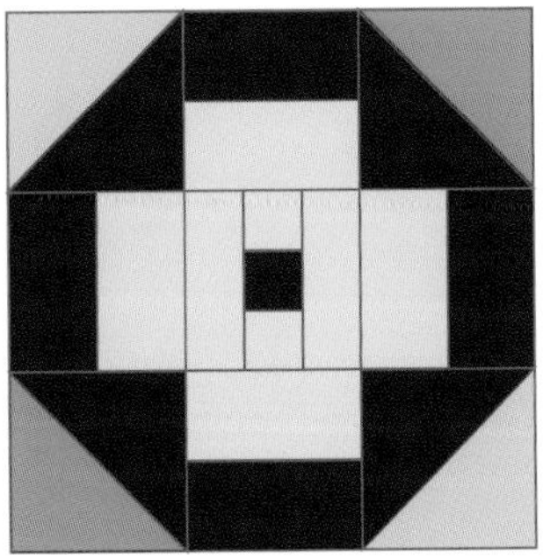

[Make 24 — 9½" unfinished blocks]

5 Join each 2″ × width-of-fabric turquoise strip to a black 2″ × width-of-fabric strip. Press to the black. From each set of matching strip sets, cut 16 — 3½″ segments. Set aside in sets of 4. You will need 24 total sets.

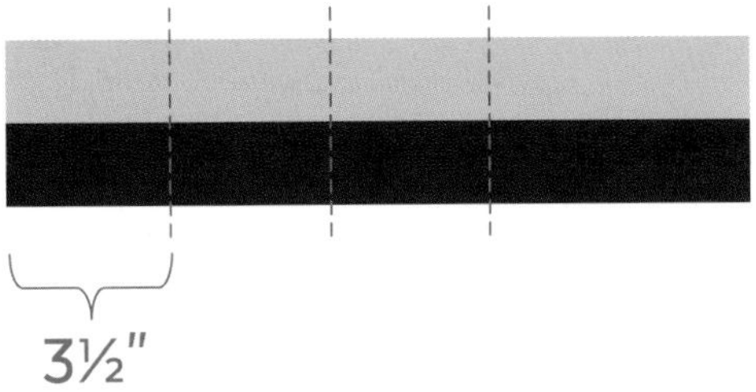

[Make 96 — 3½″ segments for turquoise blocks]

Block B Assembly

6 Assemble the blocks using 4 random orange and black half-square triangles, 1 set of 4 turquoise and black segments, and a black 3½″ square.

[Make 24 — 9½″ unfinished Turquoise blocks]

Sashing

7 To make the sashing pieces, join a black 4½″ strip to each side of a white 1½″ strip. Press to the black. Repeat to make 5 sets. Cut each pieced strip into 26 — 1½″ segments making 110 segments.

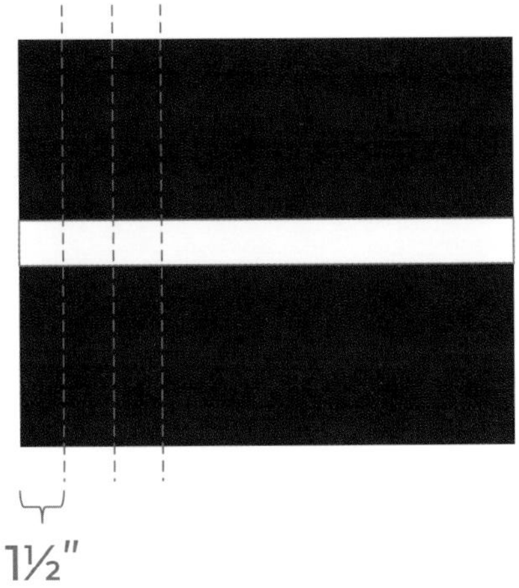

[Make 110 units for sashing]

Top Assembly

Make 8 rows consisting of alternating 3 turquoise and 3 yellow blocks joined by black and white sashing segments. Add a sashing segment to the beginning and end of each row. Make 8 rows.

[Make 8 rows]

Join 6 black and white sashing segments with a white cornerstone between each segment. Add a white cornerstone to the end of each row. Make 9.

[Make 9 rows]

Assemble the rows and sashing as shown.

Borders

Join 8 — 1½" × width-of-fabric black strips on the diagonal. Measure your quilt vertically. Cut 2 black strips to this measurement. Sew to opposite sides of the quilt. Press to the black border. Measure your quilt horizontally and cut 2 strips to this measurement. Sew to top and bottom of the quilt. Press to the black border.

Finishing

Quilting

Layer the backing, batting and top and quilt as desired. We used a variegated thread ranging from yellow to orange in a large loop-inside-a-loop design.

Binding

Join the binding strips together on the diagonal and bind.

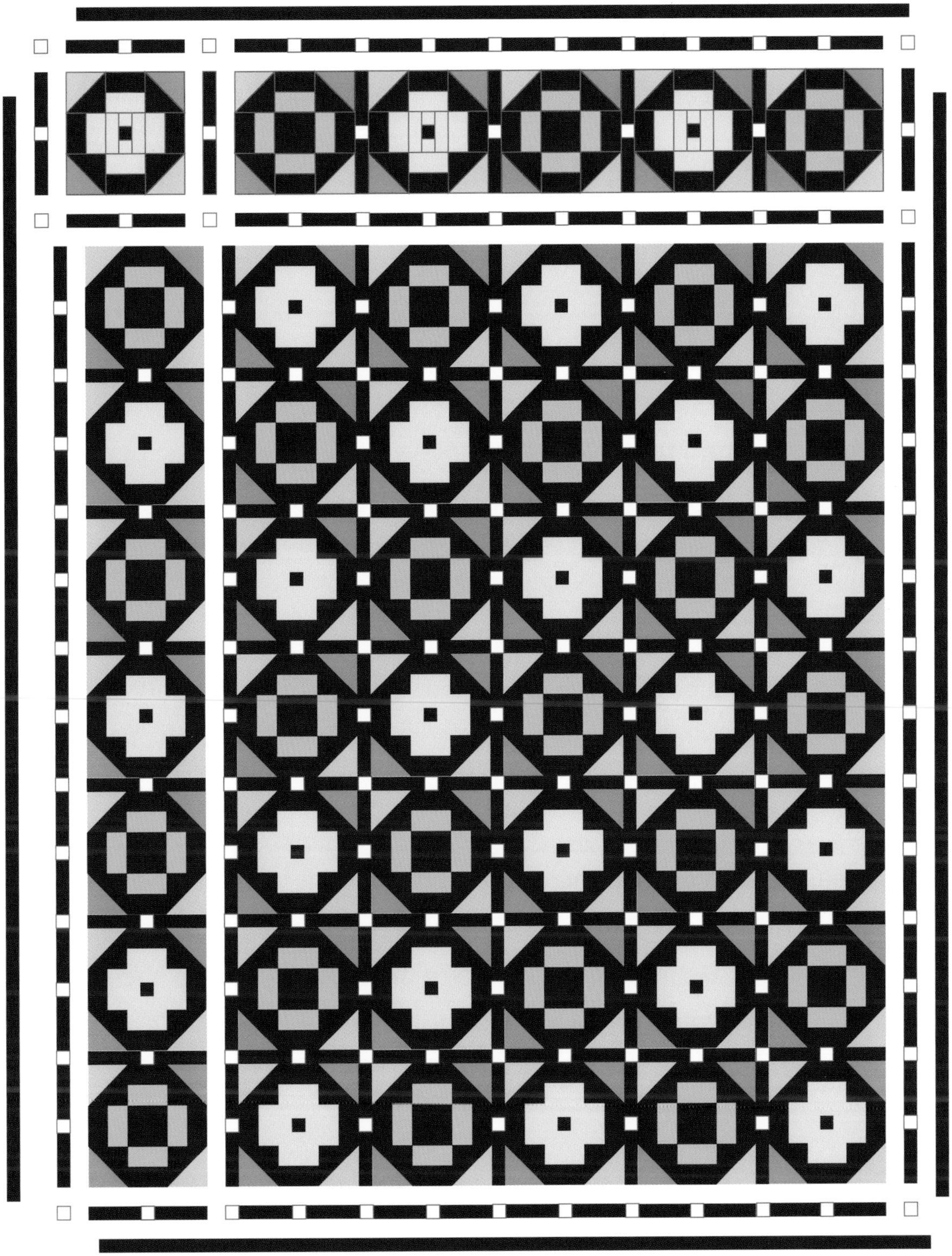

[Quilt Assembly Diagram]

Thanks to YOU!

Finished Block Size: 6″
Finished Quilt Size: 90 ½″ × 90 ½″

Our blog readers are so fun, helpful and very generous. Some time ago, we told them we were "not so bright girls," meaning we didn't have bright scraps to sew with. In no time at all readers were sending us plastic baggies full of scraps and pieces. Before long, we became "bright girls." We then asked readers to send us one strip of 2 ½″ white background fabric. They responded in full force. All of those pieces that they sent were used in the background of this quilt. We were so thankful for their generosity. Thus the name: Thanks to YOU!

We really love blogging and are so happy that it has enabled us to meet, in person or via email, so many great people — Ila, Laurel, Nell, Michelle, Debbie, Mary, Jean and oh so many others. We hope to meet many more of you.

Fabric Requirements

8 yards of various Neutrals

5½ yards of various Colored scrap prints

¾ yard total of Turquoise for binding

6 yards backing

NOTE: We save triangles from making flying geese blocks and the triangle pieces from binding strips after sewn together to make these off-kilter star blocks.

Cutting Instructions

From the various Neutrals, cut 1,804 — 2½" squares.

From the colored Prints, cut 221 — 2½" squares. The remaining colored print fabric will be used to create the star points and needs to be large enough to cover a corner of a 2½" square.

From the turquoise binding fabric, cut 10 — 2½" wide strips.

[Quick Reference Chart]

1

2½" × 2½" unfinished
884 total

2

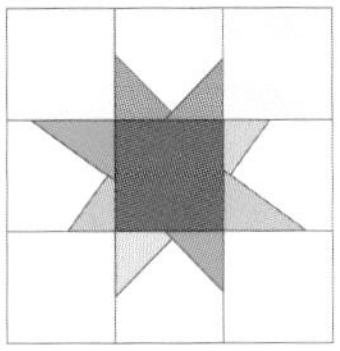

Star Block
6½" unfinished
121 total

3

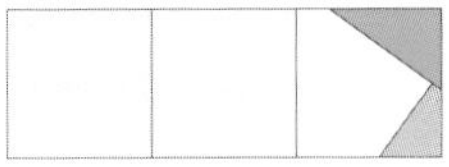

Sashing A
40 total

4

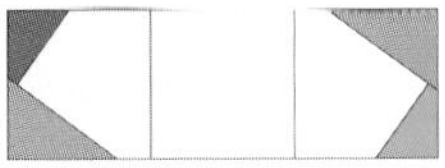

Sashing B
180 total

Sewing Instructions

Star Point Units

1 The star points will be made with a variety of scraps. Almost any size will work in making a point; however, it is very important that when the fabric is pressed back, it will cover the corner of the 2½" square.

To make a star point, place a scrap of fabric on the corner of one of the 2½" neutral squares and sew to the foundation square.

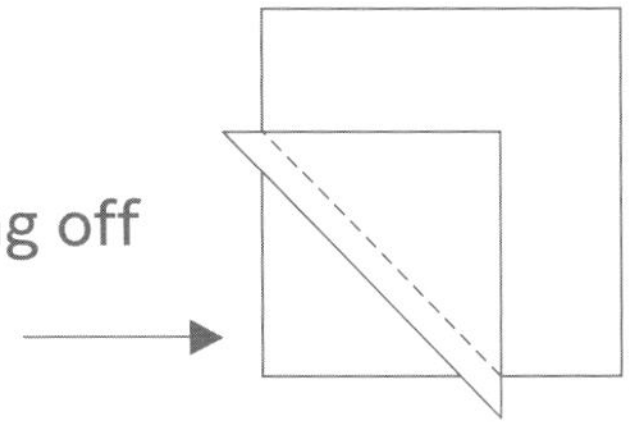

Trim the seam to ¼". Press to the colored piece.

With a second scrap, make a second star point. Make sure that when the colored scrap is pressed back, it will complete the 2½" square. Trim the seam to ¼". Press to the colored scrap.

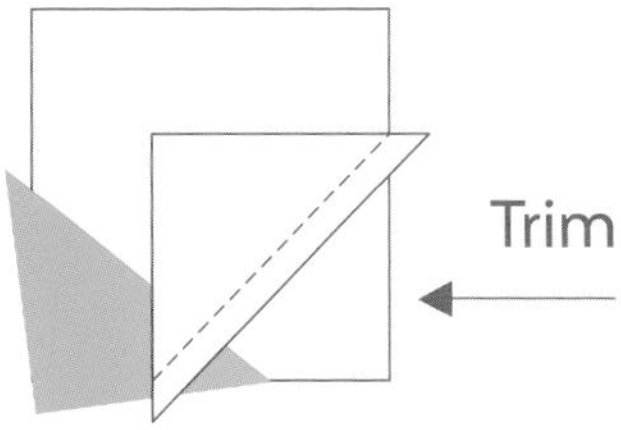

[Make 884 – 2½" star points]

Repeat the steps to create 884 star point units.

STAR BLOCK ASSEMBLY

To make one star block, you will need:

- 4 star point units
- 1 colored 2½" square
- 4 – 2½" neutral squares

2 Create the upper and lower block units by adding a neutral 2½" square to opposite sides of a star point square. Make 2. Add a star point to opposite sides of a colored 2½" square to make the middle unit. Attach upper and lower block units to middle unit. Press. Make 121 star blocks.

NOTE: The remaining stars will be created within the sashing.

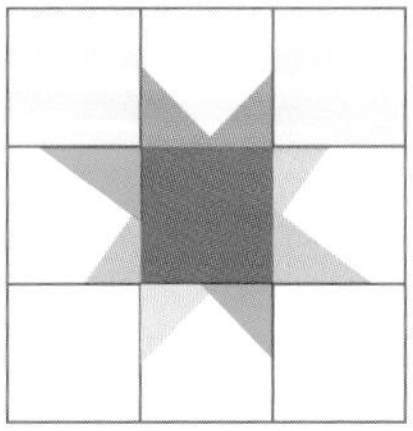

[Make 121 – 6½" unfinished Star Blocks]

Sashing A

3 Join 2 – 2½" neutral squares. Press. Join a neutral star point to the set, referring to the diagram for placement. Make 40.

[Make 40 Sashing A]

Sashing B

4 Join 1 star point to 1 – 2½" neutral square, referring to the diagram for placement. Press to the neutral square. Join a second star point to the opposite side of the neutral square, referring to the diagram for placement. Press to the neutral square. Make 180.

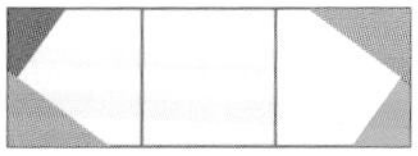

[Make 180 Sashing B]

Top Assembly

To make the side columns, join 10 Sashing A segments to 10 completed Star Blocks, making sure that the Sashing A points are all pointing in the same direction. Add an additional Star Block to the column, ensuring that the column starts and ends with a Star Block. Make 2.

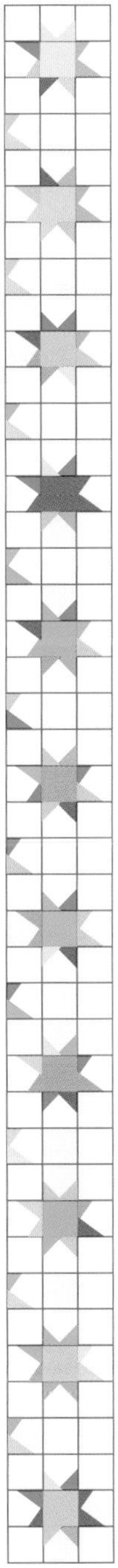

To make a vertical middle row, join a Sashing B to 10 Star Blocks. Sew the Star Block/Sashing piece sets together, creating one column. Add a Star Block to the bottom so that a pattern of star-sashing-star-sashing is made, ending with a Star Block. Make 9 columns.

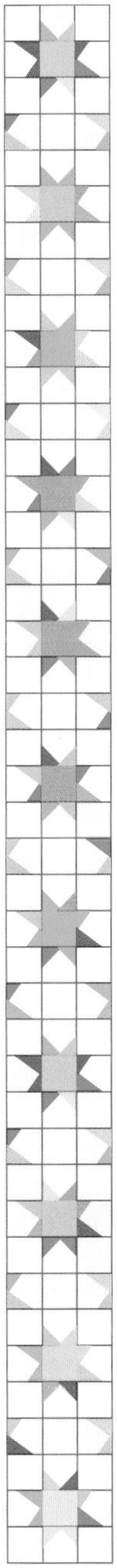

To make the vertical sashing strips, sew 1 Sashing B to 1 colored 2½″ square. Make 10. Sew together and press. Add 1 Sashing A to each end to finish the column. Make 10 columns.

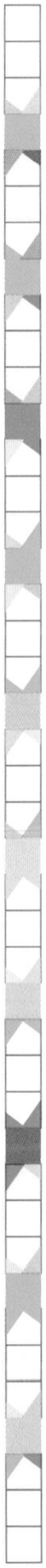

Assemble the middle of quilt by alternating star columns with sashing columns making sure to add the side columns to the outer sides.

Borders

Make the upper and lower border pieces by joining 43 – 2½" neutral squares. Make 2. Attach to the top and bottom of quilt. Make the side borders by joining 45 – 2½" neutral squares. Make 2. Attach to the opposite sides of the quilt. Press to the border.

Finishing

We used extra stars and light 2½" squares to create a pieced quilt back. Because the quilt is 90½" × 90½", 6 yards of backing wasn't quite enough fabric. Rather than buy more yardage, we made extra star blocks and cut extra 2½" neutral squares and sewed them together haphazardly in a whimsical row. We sewed a piece of backing to each side, bringing the backing piece to a usable size.

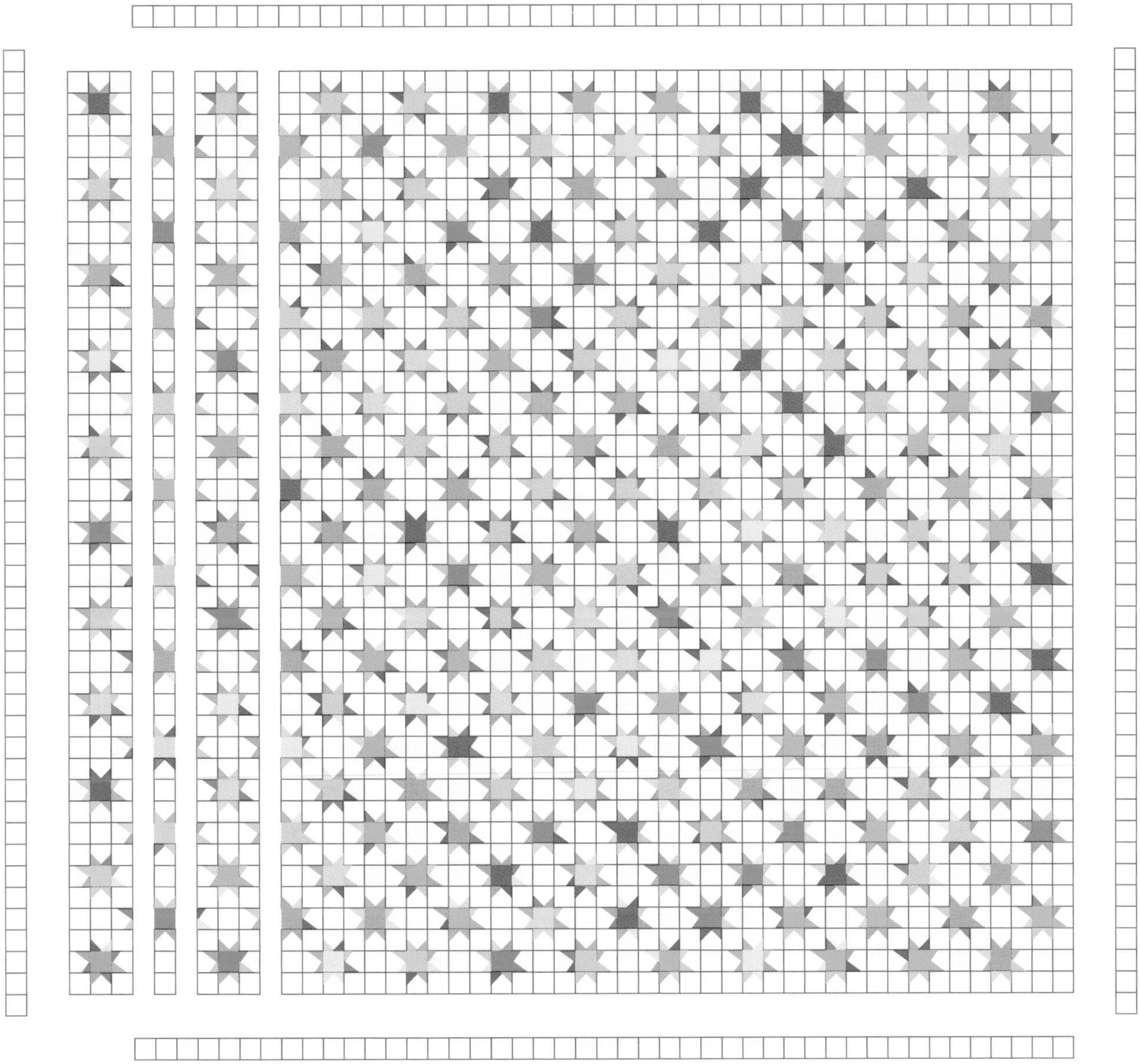

[Quilt Assembly Diagram]

Quilting

Layer the backing, batting and top and quilt as desired. We used a white thread in an overall star and loop design.

Binding

Join the binding strips on the diagonal to make 380" of binding and bind.

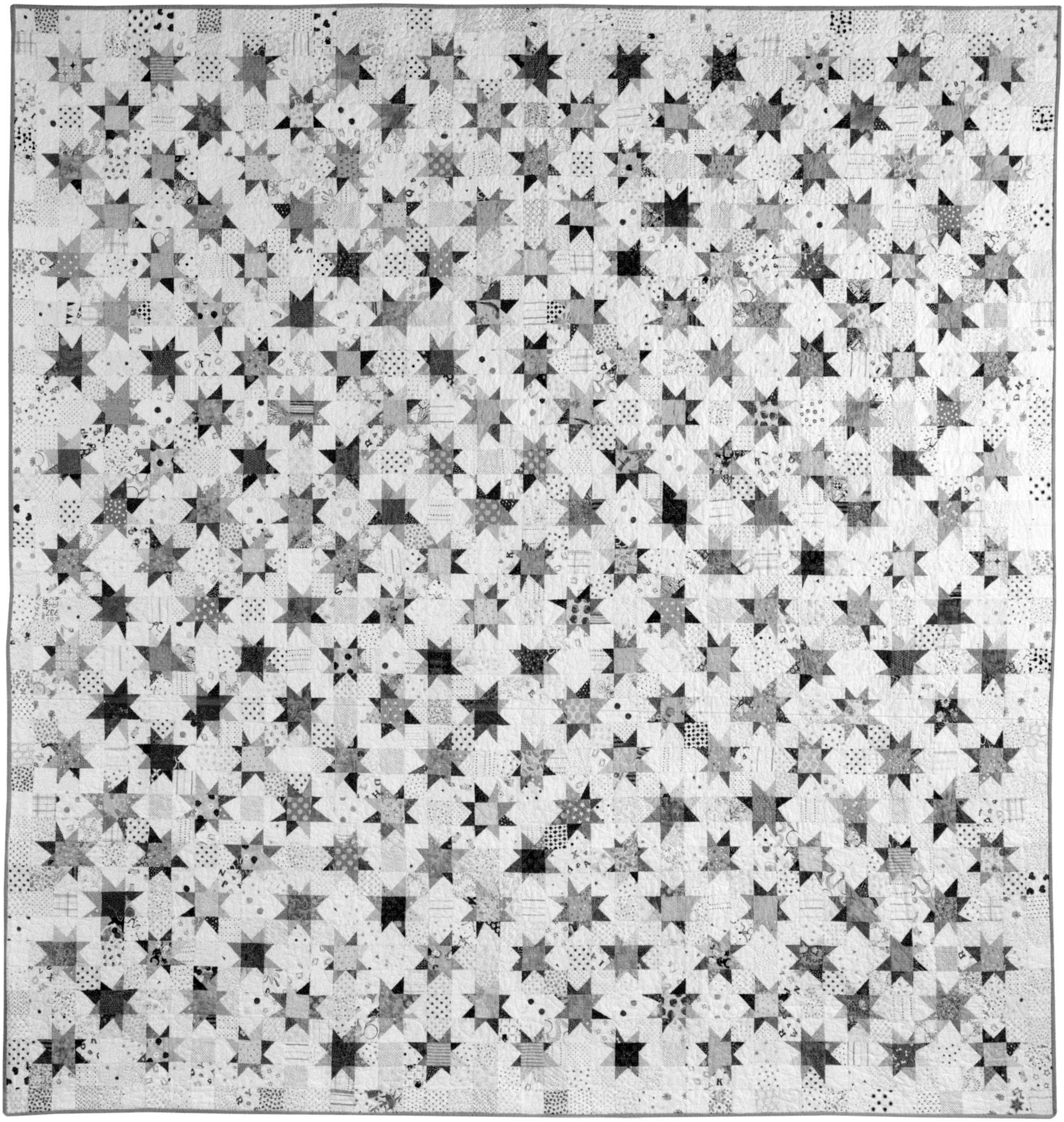

About the Authors

Jo Kramer is a dedicated wife to her farmer husband, Roger, and mother to five children. Her constant desire to maintain a family-friendly career has led to her popular blog, Jo's Country Junction (www.joscountryjunction.com). She journals about Iowa farm life; audiobooks; delicious Midwestern food; her adorable beagle, Ruby; and, most importantly, quilting.

Kelli Hanken is Jo's oldest daughter and constant weekend companion. She and her beloved beagle, Puppycat, make regular appearances on the blog. A few years ago Kelli decided to exchange "sowing her wild oats" for sewing quilts, and she has been hooked ever since. She recently married her farmer husband, Jason. While she's busy sewing quilts and chalk painting, she's also pursuing a career in nursing.

Jo and Kelli are the perfect pair as a design team. Each has a part in every quilt they create, making them quite prolific. Typically Jo designs the quilts. Kelli figures the math and pieces.

The mother/daughter duo of Kelli Hanken (left) and Jo Kramer.

Jo pieces and does the machine quilting and binding. Each is happy to pass along the quilts to the other to complete the next steps.

In addition to contributing to various publications, including *Quiltmaker, Quilty, American Patchwork and Quilting* and *Moda Bake Shop,* the two post twice daily on their blog. With the help of blog readers, they donate numerous quilts each year to local benefits and disaster relief organizations.

The mother-daughter team enjoys visiting quilt guilds and retreats. Their infectious enthusiasm and down-to-earth nature make for fun events. They treasure friendships they have made along the way and look forward to more fun in the future.

Resources

QUILTING DESIGNS

Many of the quilting designs we used are from The Pajama Quilter, Dawn Ramirez. Contact her at: www.pajamaquilter.com or email: dawn@sewdawnfun.com.

The photography for Country Girl Modern was taken at Red Barn Ranch in Harrisonville, Missouri.